T0165165

SON OF
TENANT FARMERS

THE JOURNEY

Cecil A. Brown

Copyright © 2019 Cecil A. Brown.

All rights reserved. No part of this book may be used or reproduced by any means, graphic, electronic, or mechanical, including photocopying, recording, taping or by any information storage retrieval system without the written permission of the author except in the case of brief quotations embodied in critical articles and reviews.

Scripture taken from the New King James Version®. Copyright © 1982 by Thomas Nelson. Used by permission. All rights reserved.

NIV: Scripture quotations marked (NIV) are taken from the Holy Bible, New International Version®, NIV®. Copyright © 1973, 1978, 1984, 2011 by Biblica, Inc.™ Used by permission of Zondervan. All rights reserved worldwide. www.zondervan.com The "NIV" and "New International Version" are trademarks registered in the United States Patent and Trademark Office by Biblica, Inc.™

Archway Publishing books may be ordered through booksellers or by contacting:

Archway Publishing
1663 Liberty Drive
Bloomington, IN 47403
www.archwaypublishing.com
1 (888) 242-5904

Because of the dynamic nature of the Internet, any web addresses or links contained in this book may have changed since publication and may no longer be valid. The views expressed in this work are solely those of the author and do not necessarily reflect the views of the publisher, and the publisher hereby disclaims any responsibility for them.

Any people depicted in stock imagery provided by Getty Images are models, and such images are being used for illustrative purposes only. Certain stock imagery © Getty Images.

ISBN: 978-1-4808-7729-0 (sc)
ISBN: 978-1-4808-7730-6 (e)

Library of Congress Control Number: 2019904678

Print information available on the last page.

Archway Publishing rev. date: 5/1/2019

Contents

Dedication vii

Foreword xi

Acknowledgement xiii

The Beginning 1

Early Days 5

High School 13

Basketball 18

Football 23

Tenant Farming 27

Greensboro Four and Woolworth's 31

Red Raiders Drill Team 34

Reggie Lowe, My Friend and Matchmaker 40

Beginning a Career in Monroe 51

Greensboro and Guilford County Directorship 65

Electronics Program 70

High Point 75

Shreveport, Louisiana 84

Durham 102

Coaching Youth Sports 111
The Nigeria Experience 131
Emergency Management..136
HUD Community Builders....................................149
Historic Properties, LLC......................................155
Alzheimer's 164

Endnotes...173

Dedication

After writing my memoir, I began to think about to whom I would like to dedicate this work. Two individuals came to mind, because of their impact on my life - people who loved me when I needed it the most, the two people that supported me forgave me. One is my college roommate and friend, Reggie Lowe. Not only did Reggie introduce me to my wife, but he also helped our relationship thrive until I understood that I was in love with her and wanted to spend the rest of my life with her. When I was down, he would boldly say, "after you pray, meditate for a while, then get off your knees and hustle." In other words, do not just sit and wait; you must put in the work. As my friend and roommate, Reggie, I am forever grateful to have had you in my life. Rest in peace; hold a place for me in God's Kingdom.

Ardelia Brown

The most influential person in my life has been Ardelia, my dear wife. Ardelia, this memoir is for you. Thank you for being my partner in good times and tough times. The times when you were holding down the fort while I was only there as a spectator. I looked to you to make family decisions as I found it difficult to make those family decisions without you being an active participant. I thank you for marrying me when I had nothing to offer; to move with me and our children the family that later included two children to cities like Monroe, North Carolina; Greensboro, North Carolina; Shreveport, Louisiana; Durham, North Carolina; in that order and as I write this, Wake Forest, North Carolina. Your love and your support for me is quite evident when I look back and remember that you did not hesitate when I said that I wanted to take a position in Shreveport, Louisiana, a place far away from all our family and friends. You even gave up your first teaching job to let me take us on the Shreveport journey, albeit that journey lasted only one year. You are and have continued to be the wind beneath my wings. Though your disease has changed the both of us, I'll never forget your smile and the way you called my name. Your faith in God came to light when you came to me one day and said, "Cecil, I need to tell you something," and said, "I forgive you, but I will never forget." That was over thirty-eight years ago; you have never mentioned my transgressions since. As I pen this memoir we are approaching our fifty-fifth wedding anniversary. The journey at times has been smooth and other times quite rocky, but we continued to persevere, many times traveling up the rough side of the mountain. As you began to show signs of Alzheimer's, we began to develop a new relationship, and as the disease progressed my new role became a combination of a husband and caregiver. When you were no longer able to verbally communicate, only your smile continued to show me that you still knew me as your husband.

I will forever remember the day you were sitting on your hospital bed at our daughter's house, and you looked up at me and asked, "You are going to take care of me, right?" Tears came to my eyes as I said, "Yes," then I walked away and wept. *Ardelia did not get to read this book. She passed away on December 23, 2017 at 11:35 PM. My heart is broken, but I will see you again and may your spirit watch over me and our children. Love you, Delia.*

Foreword

My wife and I enjoy attending athletic events from time to time together. When we go, we normally buy the "cheap seats", a good distance away from the court or sports field. One time, a friend connected us with tickets that were only about five rows from the field. It was a totally different experience! When you sit closer to the field, it's almost like being part of the game. Most of us live our lives in the "cheap seats" of some of America's significant events. We watch it on the news or from afar, but things often don't touch our worlds that deeply. Cecil Brown is not "most of us". He lived up close and personal as a college student and later in local government during some of our nation's most bitter and divisive times of racism and institutional bigotry.

When Cecil asked me to participate with him in this project, I was deeply honored and jumped at the chance. As a pastor, I reflect often on the Biblical proverb that says, "The glory of young men is their strength, and the honor of old men is their gray hair." That gray hair comes from a lifetime of experience and we would do well as a people to sit at the feet of Cecil Brown and others like him to receive value from that honor. Alex Haley said, "Unless we learn from history, we are destined to repeat it. This is no longer merely an academic exercise but may contain our world's fate and our destiny." There are some tragedies in this history that should not be repeated; let's do what we can to move toward a better future. Cecil shares from his personal narrative the good, the bad and the ugly of life in the Deep South and his own personal journey. When you didn't grow up in the world he did, it's easy to misunderstand the context that so many in our world face. This account will educate, inspire and motivate you as you consider the son of tenant farmers who sent nine children to college.

Pastor Eric

Acknowledgement

Eric Syfrett is an Associate Pastor at King's Park International Church. He joined the staff in 2003 as the Children's Pastor, and later moved into the role of Administrative Pastor. Ardelia served as a teacher in the Children's Ministry and it was during this time that I got to know "Pastor Eric", a young man that served the children of the church with kind words to the children and the volunteers. He and I would have lunch on occasions and as a Senior (old man) in the church I would make it my business to share words of wisdom with him, the history that is not in the history book, the words that guide us as we walk toward glory. I began by shedding my fake mask, confronting some of the painful moments of my history.

This memoir would have never been written if Pastor Eric had not taken an interest in my story. Not only did he take interest, he persevered for over two years of listening to me, taking notes, drafting and redrafting. He also encouraged me to keep talking because he kept writing.

Thank you, Pastor Eric,
Cecil A. Brown

The Beginning

I entered this world on November 20, 1941, seventeen days before the bombing of Pearl Harbor. The day that the world changed forever.

I was born into a family that consisted of my parents, Agnes and Tommie and three brothers and two sisters (one sister died as an infant), I came in as child number six and the family increased by three more brothers (one brother died as an infant) for a total of nine surviving children.

Our family was a tenant farming family. We were involved in all aspects of the farm. We did the planting, cultivating, harvesting and marketing. My father provided the seed and fertilizer. The land owner provided the land. The tobacco once sold, the land owner received one-third of the proceeds. When we harvested corn, the owner would get one wagon load out of four wagon loads of corn. My father provided the seed and fertilizer.

Our parents were able to send all nine children to college. Seven attended the Agricultural and Technical College of North Carolina, now (North Carolina Agricultural and Technical State University) in Greensboro. My oldest brother, Thomas earned a BS Degree, and was commissioned in as second lieutenant in the Air Force. He was a navigator on a KC135 refueling tanker. He retired as a Colonel. Robert graduated with a BS degree in Industrial Arts Education. He served in the US Navy on a Destroyer escort ship. In civilian life he was one of the first blacks to work in the US missile defense industry in Burlington, N.C. My sister Sadie enrolled in Home Economic at A&T and upon completing the program of study, she worked in the textile industry a few years. She would end her employment as a manager for a public housing community in Greensboro, North Carolina. Odessa graduated from A&T with a BS degree in Home Economic. She later earned a Master's Degree and would retire as the Agricultural Extension Chairman for Montgomery County, Maryland. Raymond enrolled in the Mechanical Engineering degree program and after three years he left school and retired as the manager of the management information system for a large textile firm. Cecil graduated with a BS degree in Agricultural Education and I later returned and earned a Master's Degree in Counseling and Administration. William enrolled in A&T and dropped out after two years to join the Peace Corps. He saw that as an opportunity to join a program that would make a difference in the lives of some people and for him to grow as a person. After his Peace Corps assignment, he returned to A&T and was drafted into the Army before he could enroll. After basic training he went to officer training school and was commissioned as a second lieutenant. He served a tour of duty in Vietnam as a Captain. William graduated from the University of Nebraska, Omaha. Once he retired from the military, he joined the FBI where he served for twenty plus years. Two siblings attended predominately white universities. Leslie attended the University of North Carolina, School of Law, Chapel Hill, NC; Juris 1981, University of North Carolina, School of Public Health, Chapel Hill; Master of Public Health, Health Administration, 1978, Davidson College, Davidson, NC; Bachelor of Science, Biology, 1969, Jones High School, Trenton, NC; Diploma, 1964. My youngest brother Clement graduated from Wake Forest in 1973 with a M.Ed. in Communications and N.C. Central Law, 1981: (Law) Juris Doctorate. He worked as a Home School Coordinator for the Greensboro City Schools, United States District Court for the Eastern District of North Carolina: Law Clerk to the late John D. Larkins (First African American to serve in this District's history), EEO Legal Specialist: N.C. Office of State Personnel N.C. Administrative Office of the Courts: Sentencing Services Judicial District 3B Program Director, (Craven, Pamlico and Carteret Counties), Adjunct Faculty in Communications and Criminal Law: N.C. A&T, Craven and Carteret Community Colleges, N.C. Wesleyan College, Park University and the University of Mount Olive, NC.

Back row: William, Robert, Cecil, Raymond, Thomas; Seated: Odessa, Mother, Agnes, Father, Tommie ,Sadie, Front row: Clement, Leslie

Early Days

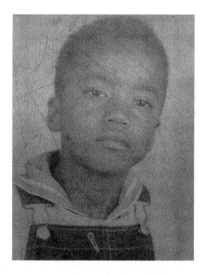

Cecil Brown 3rd Grade

As a child, for some unknown reason, I was saddled with fear: fear of airplanes, thunderstorms and even going to school. My brothers teased me about my fears. We lived near New River Air Station, a US Marine Corps pilot training base, located in Jones County, North Carolina. We could see planes on their landing approach, and it appeared as if the flight path went right over our house which was frightening to me, but not for my brothers. When planes would fly over, I would run to the house, but my brothers would hold me by my arms to keep me outside and taunt me until the plane was out of sight. Fear was a constant companion. I also had a fear of loud noises such as thunder and lightning and this fear continued until I was much older. During my early years, when a thunderstorm would start developing on the horizon, I would exhibit fear and my brothers would start teasing me. My mother was always there to call me to come in the house, even if we were in the field. When we were out priming tobacco, I had a green light from her that when a storm began to form, I could come out of the field and go to the house. There was a closed-in space under the stairs where I would go to seek refuge. Sometimes Sis Mag, my step- grandmother would join me. I never got over this fear until one day God revealed Himself to me as the one who holds the wind and the rain.

When I was in elementary school, we lived across the road from a white family, the Eubanks. They had two boys around my age. They were our playmates and during the summer months we would raid the ice boxes and warmers on the cooking stoves for food; taking bread and molasses when it was reachable.

During the school year we would get dressed for school and then play in our front yards together. Their bus would come and leave with them and we would walk to our school further down the road. On the way home they would pass us on the bus, as we were walking home. They would walk back walk to meet us and we would walk home the rest of the way together. I never recall complaining. Back then we just assumed it was right. The play time continued until we were old enough to work in the fields. When I was in the fourth grade, they moved to another farm near Pollocksville.

When we walked to school, I was the smallest child in the group, and I had to run to keep up with my brothers and sisters. I would run to catch up, fall behind and then run some more. During my first five years of school, I cried often because I did not want to go to school. As a student, I do not think I ever really enjoyed school. I always felt that I was not prepared enough, and I never felt comfortable around a group of people.

Trenton Elementary School, the "colored" school we attended, was a wooden structure. Each room contained a potbelly stove for heating purposes and wooden desks that seated two students each. During the winter months, the teacher would circle the desks around the potbelly stove and children would rotate from the front seats to the backseats so that each student would be warm. Mr. Edward Meadows, my grandfather, was the janitor at the school and was responsible for starting fires in each potbelly stove. The stoves were fueled by coal, and the teacher would select two boys to go to the coal bin behind the school to get coal when the coal bucket sitting behind the stove was empty. It was the teacher's responsibility to keep the fire burning by putting coal in the stove when needed.

Jones County Public Schools would deliver coal to replenish the bins from time to time during the winter. The coal deliveries were sporadic at best. There was a box made from wood around four feet wide and six feet long with a removal top for loading and a door to enter from the side. Sometimes the bin was essentially empty, and those students sent to the bin to bring in coal to maintain some degree of warmth had to search through the sandy bottom of the bin to retrieve lumps of coal.

I had my first and only scuffle in the coal bin. My friend, Mack Jarmon and I were sent out to bring in a five-gallon bucket of coal. We had to dig in the coal bin to find the last of the coal and we got in the scuffle over who was going to use the shovel. The teacher noticed that we had coal dust on our clothes when we returned. We told her what happened, but we did not get a punishment from her. She simply stated, "your parents will take care of you for messing up your clothes".

Our school had a large bell on the roof. A long rope extended from the bell down the side of the building, low enough for an adult or tall child to reach it. The bell was rung in the morning ten minutes before the start of class. The bell would bong at lunch time, after lunch and at the end of the day. We would begin each morning with devotions that ended with the Pledge of Allegiance and prayer, followed by a hygiene inspection. The teacher would ask for a show of hands for a volunteer inspector. She would select a student and she would inspect the student to see if the student's hands and ears were clean and if they had a handkerchief in their pocket. If one passed the hygiene inspection, then they would inspect their classmate. The handkerchief was used to clean your hands, because as we used outdoor facilities running water was not available for one to clean or dry one's hands.

In my elementary school, we had Friday movies during the last hour of the school day. One of the first movies I saw at school had a character in black face with white lips. He was singing the song: "Open the Door, Richard" and looking at me. I would move from one place to another in the room and Richard was always watching and looking at me. I was afraid and it was a long time before I watched another movie.

The students who walked to school could leave early. Raymond and I would walk home and often we would be chased by dogs along the way. I was always the one that the dog was almost ready to jump before they gave up the chase. The normal walking party from school was the Mumfords, the Meadows and the Browns. The Mumfords and Meadows lived in the town of Trenton. On Fridays, the Mumfords and the Meadows would fight as soon as we were off school grounds and out of sight of the school. The bad blood was always there, and it may still exist today.

At the end of the school day we had chores to do at home. These ranged from cutting wood for cooking and warming the sitting area of the home to bringing in kerosene from the tobacco barn which was one of my chores. One night my mother noticed that there was no kerosene in the house, she told me to go to the tobacco barn and get the kerosene and that I had to go alone. That barn appeared to be a mile away and walking in the dark terrified me! This was her way of making sure that I remembered to get it in the future to avoid another lonely, fearful trip in the dark. You will find later in this section where mother left a strong impression on me and my brothers and sisters. Things that we even talk about today…life's lessons from our first Teacher-Mother.

One summer I was working out in the field and my stomach began to hurt. Mom was convinced I was being lazy and did not want to work, but my Dad believed me and took me to the doctor. The doctor told Dad to take me to the hospital in Kinston. I had appendicitis and my appendix was removed later that day. When I woke up, my mother was sitting there praying for me. I nursed the healing process as long as I could - all the way until time to go back to school that August, to avoid any more field work that summer.

I was the shortest person in my class when we moved from elementary school to high school. I did not like it that I was always in the front of the line! A growth spurt happened during the next four years, and when I graduated high school, I was the tallest student in my class. I was also the tallest member of the basketball team my junior year.

My father and mother were firm believers in the Holy Word. They realized that memorization without understanding may not have had the same value, but those powerful words were still planted inside me from an early age. I sang in the choir at church and taught younger kids in Sunday School. Mom and Dad were really into church. From an early age, I remember that Mom and Dad were always praying; they wore out pairs and pairs of knee pads praying for the nine of us. Some of those prayers are still being answered today.

My parents modeled a generous, ordered and disciplined lifestyle to us kids even though we didn't have much. For example, most winters we would have a hog killing at the first cold snap in December and kill six or more hogs. In March, we would have a second hog killing of five or more hogs. Much of the meat from the hog killings would be made into sausage, prime cuts of hams, shoulders, and side meat would be preserved by smoking in the smokehouse on our property. The two hog killings provided more than enough meat for the family, but the killings were as large as they were because if you were a neighbor and helped in the hog killing you were compensated by being given a share of the meat products from the killings. And many times, those who did not help in the hog killings would stop by our house later in the season and ask for some meat for their family which my parents would always provide.

Another example of my parent's generosity occurred after I got my driver's license, at sixteen years old. A neighbor stopped by one day and asked my dad, "Can you let Cecil take me to Kinston to buy some coal?" My dad asked, "Do you have the money to pay for the coal?" He said, "Tommie, I was going to ask you to pay for it." My dad gave me the money for a load of coal and told me to take him to Kinston to get the coal. The neighbor had no money to pay for the coal, so dad bought it for him. My parents modeled this type of generosity of giving and helping those less fortunate throughout their lifetime.

Mom had rules. For example, one of Mom's rules was that the family car always had to be home by 11:30 p.m. I borrowed the car one Sunday afternoon, the first Sunday of our summer break from college. I drove Raymond and myself over to New Bern to a little juke joint. Raymond asked for the keys and I gave them to him, and he went somewhere else. We didn't get home that night until 12:15 a.m. Mother met us at the door and told me to give her my driver's license. I tried to tell her that Raymond had taken the car and gone somewhere else without me. In the middle of my sentence, she stopped me and said: "you asked for the car; you drove off with the car; it was your responsibility to get it back home. Give me your driver's license." Raymond was not punished. The Sunday that I was to go back to A&T after the summer break, she gave my driver's license back to me; I had to bum rides everywhere all summer long.

LIFE LESSON: If you have the responsibility, you cannot give it to someone else.

High School

From an early age and for most of my life as long as I can remember, I was compared to Raymond. Raymond was two years older than me, he was six feet four inches tall and his weight was around 190 pounds. He had a very engaging personality and he never met a stranger. It seemed that Raymond could do no wrong at home or at school and I felt that I could not do anything right.

In high school, Raymond played football and basketball. When I tried out for football my junior year, the coach gave me Raymond's jersey number and position, wide receiver. Due to fear and resentment, I developed an insecure concept of not being good enough. I couldn't jump as high, handle the ball as well as Raymond, or complete work assignments on the farm like Raymond. This wore heavily on me; why do I keep trying to compete? Teachers would also remind me of how Raymond excelled in class, and I had to measure up to the standards set by him. Looking back, I see that in some ways I embraced the situation and that the self-perceived rivalry was a motivating factor and driving force for me to succeed.

LIFE LESSON: Prove them wrong.

My parents would tell me, "If anybody can, you can. You're not better than anyone, but you are just as good as anyone."

When I entered high school in the 1955-56 school year, students from Pollocksville and Maysville were bused to Jones High School in Trenton N.C. When we graduated in 1959, there were sixty-two students in the senior class. Several students in the graduating class had been classmates from the first through twelfth grade.

During high school, I started dating a girl from Pollocksville, named Brenda. Sunday was the day I would sometime get the family car to go see her. When I drove, I would pick up four or five guys who were trying to get a ride to see their dates in Pollocksville. I became the taxi, dropping them off at their girls' houses and picking them up later. I had to be leaving Brenda's home by seven-thirty; I did not like to take Augustus, a classmate and a friend, because he did not have to leave his date's home until nine o'clock. Which meant I would wait for his departure time, sitting in the car or driving around, killing time.

For a short time, I played the trumpet in our high school band as did my friends, Augustus Cheston and Mack Jarmon. Mack and

I played trumpets. We had to carry the whole brass section alone because some students just carried instruments to look good in formation without playing but the band director made sure that Mack and I were in our place in the formation so the brass sound would be balance. When I had to choose between football and band, I gave up band.

I did continue to play in a small band that was composed of Mr. Pharaoh, our band director, on tenor and baritone sax, Mack Jarmon on trumpet, James Brit on drums, Augustus Cheston on alto sax and me on trumpet. We performed at school functions and community sponsored dances in Maysville, Pollocksville, and Trenton. We would also provide entertainment at our home basketball games. I only performed during the girls' games because I had to leave during the third quarter to join the boys' basketball team to get ready for our game.

I was also in the high school glee club. I sang tenor and I had to struggle to stay in tune. One night after a glee club event, a girl who was three years older than me grabbed my hand and said, "Where's your car?" We went outside, and she proceeded to introduce me to real sex. When we went back to the gym, she insisted that I not tell anyone. I stayed home the next day to work on the farm. The following day, when I boarded the school bus, the students in my class who rode the same bus that I did, started saying, "We know what you did the other night." And when I entered the school building everyone I met knew about "that night". She had told everyone! I found out later from other boys that she was the one that introduced them to sex as well. She dropped out of school in the eleventh grade.

Times were different back then. At my Junior Senior prom, the math teacher, Mr. Bryant saw Brenda sitting on my knee. He immediately scolded us. That Monday morning, he took me to the principal's office and recommended that I be suspended from school for a week, but the principal said, no! This day and age that kind of behavior is no big deal!

For senior prom someone bought a six pack of beer for Augustus Cheston and me. We didn't touch it. After I dropped Augustus and the girls off, I headed home and on the way, I threw the entire six pack out the car window.

Another high school memory that serves me well, was that if I had a paper to write for a class assignment and had a basketball game, I would sometimes give my younger brother, Leslie the subject matter and he would write the paper for me. He, like Raymond was considered the 'brain' in the family.

Occasionally Mr. Bryant, our math teacher, would send the girls out of class and have "father/son" talks with the guys. On one occasion he spoke to us about the tobacco farmers who went to Kinston to sell their tobacco at the warehouse. After selling their tobacco, the farmers would go to a restaurant near the warehouses and have a big steak for dinner. After they finished their meal, they would go to a grocery store and pick up neck bones to take home. Mr. Bryant told us to always "give the best to your wife and children; put yourself after them and make sure that they are taken care of." There were several other Bryant life lessons that he left with us; he was one of the many teachers who cared about us and guided us as youngsters heading to adulthood.

Jones High School class of 1959 numbers are dwindling, but we survivors are still friends. We have a reunion dinner each year and a full class reunion every five years. Our fifty-fifth reunion was held at my home in July 2015.

Basketball

One afternoon after basketball practice, the coach showed the team our new uniforms with white and blue and gold stripes. My mother found out about the new uniforms before we ever wore them and went to a Parent Teachers Association meeting and made a case that other needs for students were more important than new uniforms. Those new uniforms were not worn until new equipment was purchased for the cafeteria. My basketball team members gave me hell. We could see the uniforms, but we could not wear them.

After a few games we got to wear the new uniforms and we went on a roll, winning 23 games straight during the regular season. Even though we were the smallest school in the area, we played Atkins High School of Kinston and J.T. Barber High School of New Bern and beat both. Both teams were in Class 3A, because they were much larger. With less than three hundred students, Jones High was Class 1A.

Before the regional championship game against Fairmont High School, located in Fairmont, North Carolina, the captains of our team wrote on the chalk board in the class room which served as our locker room: "Greensboro, here we come." Which was the location where the state championship games were to be played. They were confident we were headed to the state championship final. At halftime though, Fairmont was beating our socks off. They had one kid who was six-foot eight and he was having his way with us. I was six-foot two and Smoke Berry was six-foot two. The two of us had no answer for this giant.

When the coach entered the classroom at halftime, he erased the board and did not say a word. He sat in the back of the room and only spoke when he said it was time to go, because halftime was over. We went back fighting in the second half and James Kornegay, J.W. Willie and Jesse (Shine) Moore had the second half of a lifetime. We won in a cakewalk.

Years later in August 1959, Melvin, the six-foot eight player from Fairmont's team entered A&T the same time I did; we reminisced about our first meeting that night at Fairmont's gym and that was the beginning of a friendship.

Our team's first game in the state playoffs was against York Road of Charlotte. We beat them easily, with James Kornegay scoring forty-two points that morning. Atkins High and J.T. Barber High School were there for the Class 3A State Tournament, preparing to warm up as we came off the floor from beating York Road.

Even though we had trounced both Atkins High and J.T. Barber High School during the regular season, they were competing again since they were in the larger classification.

The team was housed in Scott Hall, a men's residence hall on the campus of NC A&T State College (now NC A&T State University). Our basketball team was made up of guys from three towns: Trenton, Pollocksville and Maysville. Our first game of the tournament was against York Road out of Pineville North Carolina. We beat them easily. The team had dinner in the dining hall on campus and then we retired for the night. A discussion started among the players about James' scoring in the game; James and Jessie Shine Moore were from Trenton. The Pollocksville and Maysville guys claimed James had been hogging the ball to get a new state record of 42 points. That discussion soon became pushing and shoving and later throwing trash cans full of water on each other. Our coach was nowhere to be found; the team had some idea where he was and with whom, but we never asked, and he never said. With no adult supervisor around that night, the "team" was lost.

We started the game out of rhythm and we never recovered, the coach kept asking us what was going on and why we weren't communicating on the floor. The flow and rhythm of the game did not exist. Our first bad game out of twenty-six and we lost to Jordan Sellers High of Burlington N.C, who went on to win the State Championship in 1958. We all believed that, had the coach been in place that night, he probably could have addressed our issues (or at least shut down the fights) and put the team back together; we were confident there would have been a different result.

The next morning our chaperone/driver was hungover, smelling like alcohol and he asked me to drive his car home from Greensboro to Trenton, NC. I had just turned sixteen in November 1957 and this happened in March 1958. In the back seat of the car were Hardy Lynn Brown, Bender Berry and Adolphus Harris. The drive was around one-hundred and eighty miles. When I got home and told my mother, she hit the ceiling, "Why did you drive? You know you should not have driven that far. What was wrong with him? I will have to have a talk with that man!" and she did!

My senior year in high school, our basketball team won only fifteen games and therefore did not make the playoffs. Hardy Hall was a member of our high school basketball team, we were the only seniors on the team. During basketball season on game nights, Hardy would come home with me. We would have dinner and wait for the time to go to the gym or catch the bus for away games

Bayboro, North Carolina, a small town, north east of Trenton, North Carolina in Pamlico County, won it all. They beat us three times with a key player, named Joe Embry, a transfer from New York. In May 1959, I graduated from high school; I was accepted to and entered North Carolina A&T College in Greensboro, North Carolina. Joe Embry and I met again at A&T in August 1959. He reminded me often of those three games where he had kept us out of the playoffs.

Football

The Monday after the return from the state championship game, Mr. Wynn told me I was to play football in the fall of 1958 because I needed to get a little more physical for basketball. During the summer, my brothers and I threw around the football when we had a chance. I went out for the team that fall and won a spot as the starting wide receiver. Our first game was with J.T. Barber High School in New Bern.

As we were dressing for the night game, Mr. Wynn was issuing uniforms. When he called my name, I was given number 97; Raymond had worn number 97. My first game was one of my best games. As a first-time starter, I caught at least six passes on one drive; Hardy Lynn Brown, my cousin and quarterback, kept calling my number. We became a winning team that year. Yet, we did not make the playoffs because two of our better players, the starting quarterback (Hardy Brown) and our starting halfback, (Roy Lee Barber) were put off the team because they violated team rules.

Hardy Hall and I were the only seniors that played both basketball and football. He missed two football games that year; in both games, I played my regular offensive end position and Hardy's normal defensive end position. My first time at defensive end, the screen passing ran me crazy and the second time the coach told me to take the tackle spot and tell Tyrone Gooding, the tackle, to move over to the right end spot. The opposing team was running the power sweep and Tyrone was bigger and stronger than me. Tyrone did not move out to the end position and, when the play started, I jumped into the end spot and got cut down by the lead half-back. I laid on the ground watching as they scored. Our playoff chance went down on that power sweep.

Hardy Hall, my lifelong friend, and I met in the fourth grade, we were classmates. He spent his first three school years at a small one room Jones County school in Comfort, North Carolina. In high school, Hardy missed a lot of days from school because, like many other children, he had to stay home to work on the farm. Hardy's parents were sharecroppers and some landowners required that their tenants keep their children at home from school to help on the farm until the harvest season was completely over. So, for some students, school attendance was sporadic, at best, from the beginning of the school year in late summer until mid to late October. I believe Hardy's parents knew the importance of education for their children, but likely found themselves in an untenable position of choosing between acquiescing to or defying the expectation of the landowner who could "let the tenant" go for any or no reason.

During our ninth-grade year, I started to send class assignments to Hardy when he was out; I would send notes to him by his sister, Velma. When one of our teachers announced a test day, I would send a note to Hardy telling him of the date. He would come to school on test days and, on most test, he would be one of the top scorers. On test days if Hardy was supposed to stay home, he would sometimes hide from his father and when the school bus was pulling away from the house he would run and catch it to school. Because of his family's farming situation, Hardy often was unable to purchase textbooks or supplies at the beginning of the school year. He seldom had paper, pencil, or even lunch money. Hardy was loved by all his classmates and all of us were willing to help by sharing with him.

After high school, Hardy moved to New York, like so many high school seniors of my generation and before. He found work in a hospital washing dishes. He told me that it was during this time that the hospital started to install computers; when he had a break in his duties in the kitchen, he would go to the computer room and watch and ask questions. Eventually the person in charge of computers hired Hardy. He had a very successful career and could provide for his family. He later retired as the manager of the data center and as a consultant at another hospital.

Hardy was a gifted man but would have been held back by circumstances. His initiative to go to that computer room during the installation opened a door that became a source of favor from God. We had a break in our communications because when I was consumed by alcohol, I cut ties with almost everyone. When I would go home my mother would tell me that Hardy stopped by and asked about me and shared with her what he was doing.

At Hardy's last class reunion, that was held in Norfolk Va. at the home of Isaiah Hill, another high school classmate, he told us that his doctors had said that his medicine was no longer helping control his cancer and there was nothing else they could do. His last gift to himself was a trip to Graceland with his family. He passed away a few months later. At his funeral I was given the opportunity to speak for our class. My comments were centered around memories of days gone by and our friendship. I ended by saying, "you do not need another pencil." Rest in peace, my friend.

LIFE LESSON: When opportunity meets ability, good things happen.

Tenant Farming

William and Cecil

My daddy would recount the time early on in our family landlord/ tenant arrangement with Julien "Old Man" Warren. Old Man Warren approached him in the field one day and suggested that he keep my oldest brother Thomas out of school to help on the farm. Daddy said his response to Old Man's suggestion was:

"Mr. Warren, you would not keep your son, Julien, out of school to help you do your work and I don't know why you would expect me to keep my son out of school to do mine!" Daddy said that issue was never brought up again between Old Man Warren nor with his son, Julien II, after he took over as landlord. Believe me, not all landlords would have accepted a rebuff from a Negro tenant as Old Man Warren did.

We were one, if not the only, tenant family that was not a fifty-fifty farmer; this was an arrangement where the tenant got half, and the landlord got half. We were a one fourth, three fourths tenant, with the landlord getting one fourth and we were getting three fourths. During corn harvesting season, Raymond and I would increase our portion by increasing the volume of the wagon. We used six large ears of corn and put them in the sides of the wagon to raise the sides by five inches. This increased the total volume of our three wagon loads. On Mr. Warren's one wagon, we would take the ears of corn out thereby decreasing his allotment. We knew what we were doing was wrong and we never told our Dad.

On the Sunday morning I left for college, I asked my dad for my tuition and he said to me, "I did not think you were going to college. I thought you were going to stay here and help on the farm. You had not told me that you were going." I did not know what to say. I finally said, "I told Mother."

He looked at me and said, "How much do you need?" I told him one thousand dollars and he reached in his pocket and gave me the money I needed plus a few dollars extra.

After we finished breakfast, he took me to Kinston to catch the bus for Greensboro. My only possessions were a radio and a suitcase with clothes. The colored section of the bus was filled, but the white section was not. Charles Leonard from Kinston was going to A&T College too. I stood in the bus aisle behind him. We stood for at least an hour until the bus arrived in Goldsboro, NC where a few colored people got off the bus and we took their seats. Little did I know what I was heading into and how my life would change in a short period on time. Little did I know when I left home, that in less than a year I would be involved in demonstrations concerning civil rights. The sad thing is I knew that inequities existed, but I never dreamed of being a part of a historic movement and witness to such a change.

Only four students of my class of seventy-two went to college in the fall of 1959; some left for New York, Washington D.C., and other points north. Some even left after the graduation exercise on Sunday and were on a job the following Monday morning. For example, Jason White went on a construction job with his uncle that Monday. Jason made a career in the construction industry and retired as a construction manager having managed the construction on some of the largest developments in the Northeast. Others later went to college and on to nursing and other professions.

After my first quarter, I had a 1.86 average. I had graduated high school with an A plus average, but I had difficulty adjusting to college life. I had planned to major in Chemistry when I went to A&T, but my first quarter grade for chemistry was a "D". That December, I went to talk to Mr. J. I. Barber, a professor and counselor, and a native of my home town. He told me after our discussion that I just needed to relax, "With your study time, give special study to your difficult classes and see what the next quarter looks like."

I was still ready to give up when I left him and went to my room. I packed my bag and called the bus station and asked, "When does the next bus leave for Kinston, North Carolina?" The next bus was at 3:00 p.m. I sat on my suitcase looking out the window thinking about home and what I was going to say and what was I going to do if I went home. Tobacco flashed through my mind and the scorching heat of the tobacco season. That reminder was enough to persuade me to push through the difficulties in college. I stood up, unpacked my clothes and went to register. When I registered, I changed my major to Agricultural Education, the same as my oldest brother, Thomas, who at that time was a First Lieutenant in the Air Force.

Greensboro Four
and Woolworth's

One day, I was sitting in my Scott Hall dorm room, when Ezell Blair, Jr., Joe McNeil, David Richmond and Franklin McCain, guys who roomed two doors down from me, walked in and started talking about what happened at Woolworth's. The day was February 1, 1960, they were talking about the start of the lunch counter sit-in which opened a new front in the emerging national civil rights movement.

A large number of students from campus got involved on campus and in street marches; we saw firsthand the power of peaceful resistance. We all believed that demonstration and protest in the streets of Greensboro would help to bring about change. There had been talk about some acts of civil disobedience in the dormitory before the action on February 1, 1960.

Word circulated in our dormitory that an incident happened to Joe McNeil on a return trip from his home in New York, which helped incite the Woolworth's sit-in. Joe had gone home for a family visit and on his return to Greensboro, the bus stopped at the bus station in Richmond, Virginia. The lunch counter at the station would not serve him food at the counter. The word is that when he entered Scott Hall, he went to his room and discussed possible courses of action with Blair, McCain and David Richmond. It was at this time McNeil said, "We have to take action," and it was decided that Woolworth's would be the target.

A&T students purchased goods and supplies from Woolworth's but were not allowed to eat at the lunch counter. The four freshmen continued to sit at the Woolworth's lunch counter until the store closed that night, protesting the policy of no blacks were allowed to sit at the lunch counter and eat. You could order off to the side of the counter and take food out, but not sit and eat. Over the next few days the crowd grew and the ladies from Bennett College and The Women's College (now University of North Carolina at Greensboro) joined the sit in movement.

One afternoon, Woolworth was crowded and the ladies from Bennett College and the Women's College had entered Woolworth and were sitting and standing at the lunch counter, where they were yelled at by some white men. At this time, twenty plus A&T College football players walked in and took a stance between the women and the yelling white men. The football players escorted the women out of the building and saw to it that they were placed in cabs to take them back to their College.

During the times of protesting, on Sundays at A&T would serve only breakfast and lunch and a brown paper bag with a sandwich and fruit provided by the dining hall; students marched downtown and then returned to campus. We heard that a number of student protesters were being held in an agricultural building on the east side of Greensboro because the jails were at capacity. We marched out to the site and began to sing. Jesse Jackson, who transferred from Ohio to A&T in the fall of 1960, was one of the students being held in the facility. He interrupted the singing with a prayer and preaching, like only a Baptist preacher could deliver. He moved the spirit of all the students that day and I think we all believed that we were doing God's work.

One week after the Greensboro sit-ins had begun, students in other North Carolina towns launched their own sit-ins. Demonstrations spread to towns near Greensboro including Winston Salem, Durham, Raleigh and Charlotte, as well as Lexington, Kentucky and across other southern States. To have been a part of and a witness to this civil disobedience demonstration, I must admit, had a profound impact on my life and changed my views of the world around me. As I entered the world of work, I know that I was more aware and paid attention to individuals and the action of whites, as you will see in the ensuing Chapters.

Red Raiders Drill Team

My freshman year, I wanted to be in the marching band, but there were no brass instruments available. I had left my trumpet at home and my brother Clement had started playing it, so I tried out and was selected for the Air Force ROTC Red Raiders Drill Team instead. Raymond was also on the team, so here I was again, living in his shadow. There I met guys who would remain friends for life. When I went out for a tryout, I was familiar with most of the drill movements because Raymond had been on the team for two years. He had taught my brothers and other guys who worked as day laborers in the tobacco fields the movements when he was home during the summer. We would perform the routines at the end of tobacco rows and in the dirt paths leading to the fields. Charles Leonard joined the Air Force ROTC drill team and we became life-long friends.

I interrupt this with a typical summer day during tobacco harvesting time in 1960.

July 9, 1960
Route 1, Box 7A, Trenton NC

It is July 9, 1960 at 4:30 am and Tommie Brown is waking us up. Time to get the day started! First, we had to take tobacco out of one barn to take it to the pack house. With two oil burning lanterns to light the barns in hand, Daddy pulled the trailer up to the barn and put the lanterns in strategic places for maximum light. Raymond took the bottom tiers and I went up to the top. I always liked the top because I would only have to handle half of the tobacco. The bottom person was responsible for taking the top person's stack of tobacco and giving it to the person on the ground. Once the trailer is filled from the barn of tobacco, we will take it to the pack house and unload it. It is now 5:45 am.

6:00 am - I wash my face and hands, brush my teeth and eat breakfast. Now the day really begins. I go out to the mule lot to feed the hogs and water them, and then get Mickey, the mule, ready to go to work. I first put on the bridle and made sure the bits are in her mouth, then the collar, checking the line from the bits, through the collar. Finally, I hooked her to the first tobacco truck for the day. Dad would leave to pick up the field hands and the stringers (the workers who move the tobacco from the trucks and string it to be placed in the curing barn).

On this day, I along with two of my brothers go to the field and begin priming, or cropping the tobacco and filled two trucks before the barn workers arrived. This way we would keep the barn workers busy with not much down time, the primers would not have to rush, and we could work at a smooth pace.

Around 10:30 am the truck driver would bring us soft drinks and a snack. Today it is a Pepsi cola and an oatmeal cookie. This break lasted about ten minutes and I was back between the rows of tobacco, flanked by five others on my left. We are in the second week of harvest and my back is still not ready for this bending. We will be able to stand to prime the tobacco because it will be so tall in two more weeks. The conversations in the field centered around sports and girls.

We took a quick two-minute break for Raymond to show us how to do a Crazy Baby: a maneuver that the NC A&T Red Raiders performed. The temperature is now 90 degrees and humid. Hope it does not rain today, a quick afternoon shower followed by the heat will cause our wet shirts to heat up and the steam will make for an uncomfortably hot afternoon.

At 11:45 am, we stop for lunch. Dad would take the workers home for lunch, then come home, eat lunch and take a power nap on the couch. At 12:45, Dad is back on his way to Trenton to pick up the hands. I am hooking Mickey back up and heading back to the fields; we will prime tobacco today until 4:30 pm.

Then we go to the barn and fill two barns from today's harvest. The workers are taken home. I take Mickey to the barn and make sure she has water and feed for the night. Then I go to the house, wash up, and eat dinner. At 6:30, I can now sit down to watch Walter Cronkite on the CBS Evening news. At 10pm, it is time for bed; 4:30 am will be here soon. WHAT A DAY!

After it was known that I was Raymond's brother, I was moved among the returning squad members. My fellow freshmen did not know that I knew the steps until I was sent to work with the returning team members. I then started teaching freshman team members the routines, especially my roommate Reggie Lowe. He was hell-bent on making the team because one of his high school classmate was on the Army Drill team.

It was also during my freshman year that I took my first real drink. The drill team was on our way to Nashville, Tennessee to participate in the half time activities during a football game between A&T and Tennessee State University. One of the drill team members had smuggled some wine on the bus; the bottle was being passed around. I took a big drink and I loved it. Each time there was wine around during drill team events, I would take a drink. It was during my sophomore year that I started to smoke, a bad habit that I maintained for thirty years.

Once when the drill team participated in a parade in Reidsville, North Carolina, Raymond was the commander and three white girls were following us along the parade route. After about four blocks, one of them just yelled out, "Lord, those are some pretty N....ers;" we all laughed. Raymond called out the cadence "Cream Step" to get us back in step; we moved on down the street with the girls still with us.

There was a night that we found out that God really watches over us while we are still sinners. On this occasion as the drill team was driving back from homecoming parade in Clinton, North Carolina, Sergeant Ware was driving a small bus with twenty team members. I was driving a military issued station wagon with seven cadets behind him and Berry Taylor was with four cadets. Barry was driving his personal car behind me. Berry and I were following some distance behind the small bus.

I slowed down because the car in front of me was going very slow. We were on a two-lane road; Berry was behind me and we both pulled to the left lane to pass at the same time. I accelerated to avoid a collision, but so did Berry. Our cars touched at my rear wheel panel but didn't seem like there was any real damage. Berry slowed down and I moved back to the right. We drove the rest of the way back to campus, without stopping. I dropped the cadets off that were in my car and I then took the car where it was stored each night. I met Sergeant Ware there and told him what happened; he looked the car over and saw no real damage. He said, "Good night and I will see you at practice tomorrow".

LIFE LESSON: God covers us with the blood that He shed for our sins.

I was a member of the drill team for four years; three years as a squad leader and one year as the commander. Each year we were selected to attend the Cherry Blossom Festival that is held in Washington, DC in early April. For two years, we were third in the nation among both Air Force and Army teams. My senior year, the year I served as commander, I had a squad of freshman and sophomores and the team won first place in the Air Force and second place overall.

Reggie Lowe, My Friend and Matchmaker

Cecil and Ardelia

I first saw Reggie on stage during the freshman talent show at A&T in September 1959. He was singing "Please, Please, Please" by James Brown. The crowd was on their feet screaming as if James Brown himself was in the room - I think because of his moves, not so much his voice. The next day he was at drill team practice and he and I talked about my knowing the Drill Team short precision movements.

For the next few weeks we spent time together after practice learning and mastering the routines. Our friendship just grew, and we became roommates at the beginning of the second quarter of our freshman year. We were roommates for three years.

Reggie started out majoring in industrial arts, then changed his major to the trade of Electrician, planning to become an Electrical Contractor. His goal was to work for Con-Edison in New York. Reggie was dating Jeanne, his high-school sweetheart who became a nurse; he made it known that she was his girl and that as soon as he finished college, he was going to New York to marry her. He did just that.

When the Red Raiders flag bearer gave up the position at the end of the first quarter of our freshman year, Raymond was the commander. He announced that he would be holding a tryout for the open flag bearer position. Reggie told me as we walked to our dorm that he was going to be the next flag bearer for the drill team. For a few nights before the tryout, he would practice routines with our broom. He became the flag bearer as a freshman which had never been done before, and he held the position for the two years that he was on the team.

Reggie was from a small town in North Carolina named Magnolia and the Army drill team's flag bearer was Vernal Stalling, from Magnolia as well. They had been high school classmates, which made for very good competition between the two and great showmanship for both teams. Like most roommates during our time in college, Reggie and I would bring a box of food back from home after weekend visits or holidays. We shared those boxes and when one of us had five dollars we shared it. We would even, on occasion, wear each other's clothes.

I made sure that Reggie's Red Raider drill team boots were spit shined, even if I had to shine them myself. One Friday night, the band he sang with had an engagement and I noticed that his boots needed a good spit shine because we had a drill meet that Saturday morning. Once I finished shining my boots, I shined his and set them on his bed. The image of the team had to be protected, because we didn't need any demerits.

Reggie graduated and left to start a new life in New York with Jeanne. They would add two sons to their union, Reggie Jr., and Wendell. Reggie would never work for Con-Edison; however, he started his own electrical business named Lowe and Sons and as he would say sometimes, he lit up New York!

Over the years, we would talk just to catch up and sometimes just to cry on the other's shoulder. When I wanted to or felt the need to pour my issues out, I would call Reggie and likewise he would call me. All our conversations were never filtered, always telling it like it is. Love and respect afford you that privilege.

A few years before Reggie passed, Ardelia and I went to his home in Brooklyn, N.Y. Before we left, he and I made our final commitment to each other: that the last survivor would speak at the other's funeral. When Reggie passed in December of 2015, I honored that commitment. At the funeral, I spoke to his family and friends about the Reggie that I knew and the Reggie that I loved like a brother and a very good friend. I think of him often. (Reggie, Jr. told my daughter that he will speak at my home going.) Fifty-two years of friendship. When I call now to check with Jeanne, she says, "Bud, I am doing the best I can." I have never asked her why she calls me Bud.

Ardelia Brown

During my sophomore year, August of 1960, Reggie came in the room one day with a message from a young lady name Ardelia Perdue. Reggie gave her the nickname "Doo Doo", based on the second half of her last name; no one other than Reggie could call her that. She had asked him who I was and told him that she would like to meet me.

I was still talking with Brenda back home and at that time, I was not really interested in meeting another girl. She continued to send messages through Reggie and when I walked across campus to class, she and her friends would at times be hanging out their dorm window calling my name. It got to the point that I would walk the long way to class just to avoid her. She was a majorette and a freshman at the time.

Eventually, Reggie said that he was not going to deliver any more messages. One day, Reggie and I were walking to the dining hall for dinner and we met Ardelia and her friend, Gussy. We stopped and had a conversation, and after a brief period, Reggie and Gussy walked off and left the two of us together. Ardelia and I went to dinner together and we walked the campus that night until her curfew.

We continued our after-dinner walks over the next few months and spent time together after Drill Team and Band practice, strolling around campus, holding hands and having long passionate kisses. The evening after the homecoming game, I invited Ardelia to go with me to a house off campus. As we walked in the house, I received permission to go upstairs. Before we reached the room though, a policeman came in and began to question the two of us along with the owner of the house. As Reggie was entering the house, he and I made eye contact and I motioned for him to leave.

Ardelia and I were taken downtown Greensboro, booked, and jailed (charges: occupying a room for immoral reasons). Allen Goins was a student at A&T and a Greensboro police officer, although I didn't know it before this occurred. He just happened to be in the jail area when I was being placed in jail; he asked me what was going on and the officer told him. He said to me quietly, "I will have you out in a few hours." I told him that I did not know where Ardelia was and he said he would find her. I used my single phone call to call my brother Robert in Burlington, N.C.

Allen got us released and took us back to campus. He also said that he placed our arrest report someplace where the newspaper reporters would not see it the next morning. He did that because he knew that if our arrests were found out by A&T officials, we would have been expelled from school. That night, before Ardelia went into her dorm, we decided that if we were expelled, we would try to transfer to Florida A&M University, in Tallahassee, Florida.

When I entered the second floor of Scott Hall, in the hallway by my room, Reggie was sitting on the floor by the door. When he saw me, he got up and came down the hall to meet me and said, "Man, I am glad to see you!" I told him what happened and that I was afraid that Ardelia and I would be put out of school when it hit the newspapers. The next day, my brother Robert retained Attorney Errata Johnson to handle our legal matter. She settled the matter and the event never reached the eyes of A&T officials who had the power to expel us. After that ordeal Ardelia and I agreed that we would not be going to any more off campus private homes. Car rides and long walks were our romantic excursions.

One night, there was a social event at Cooper Hall. Brenda was in Greensboro, and I had told her about the social, but I had already invited Ardelia to go with me. I was drinking before the event with Reggie, Wesley Brown, and several other teammates. After they left, I went to sleep. When I woke up, I decided to go downstairs to the social. I took a quick shower and headed to the event. Ardelia was at the event and a little upset because I had not picked her up. We began to talk, and she got over her disappointment of my being late to the party. About that time, Brenda walked in with my cousin and her husband. Brenda came up to me and as I was about to introduce her to Ardelia, Ardelia reached for her high heel shoe and tried to hit me.

Immediately, Reggie and Wesley took me out of the social and back to my room. Reggie went back and took Ardelia to her dorm. The next day, I was walking through campus and it looked as if everyone knew about the incident that happened in Cooper

Hall's basement the night before. Ardelia and I made up and began to grow in our relationship, even talking about a future together. One night, while we were walking across the campus, we agreed that the name of our first child would be Stephanie.

One year later, on December 14, 1962, Ardelia and I were married in Greensboro with two friends, Wesley Brown and Carolyn Howard, serving as witnesses. We spent our first night of marriage in a black owned motel on Gorrell Street in Greensboro. Raymond Carver had his own car and he was our driver that night. We had not told our families, so on December 16, 1962, she went home to Eatonville, Florida and I went home to Trenton, N.C.

A week later, when we returned from the Christmas break, my sister Sadie contacted me and told me I had some mail at her house. I had used her address for the marriage license and a copy of the license had come to her house. We then told everyone, including the university. Once the university was notified, we had marriage privileges. Even though we were still housed in separate dorms, she could come and go as she pleased if she checked out with me. It is interesting that our grade point averages went up after we got married.

During the early spring of 1963, Ardelia and I, along with my brother Robert and his wife Barbara and their child, went to Trenton, N.C. Ardelia was introduced to my mother and father, and my two brothers, Leslie and Clement, who were still at home. My father said to me, "She is a pretty little thing". My mother said, "Now don't go doing like Raymond and drop out of college."

I was determined to finish school when Ardelia and I married. Ardelia dropped out when she got pregnant before her senior year but returned to A&T when Stephanie was three years old.

After Christmas, I was assigned to do student teaching at Little River High School in Durham, North Carolina in the spring of 1963. Each day, I would have my lunch in the classroom shop and, before I could finish my lunch, a small group of female students would come to the shop to smile and ask questions. I was twenty-one and they were seventeen and eighteen. That student teaching experience convinced me that I was not cut out to be a high school classroom teacher. The needed preparation, management of student conduct and confinement in the school all day was not for me. This led me to pursue a career with the agricultural extension service instead.

On one occasion during my student teaching, I rode from Durham to Greensboro and back with a John Bullock a teacher from Little River School in Durham County. I was assigned student teaching to complete a course requirement to become a teacher. I stopped by Brenda's work place to tell her that I was married and to wish her well. She was upset when I told her; she kept asking, "Why?" She said to me, "When they told me that you were here, I thought you were coming back to me." I told her that I did not mean to hurt her and walked out. The last words I heard from her that day was, "Why? Why?"

I had to go to summer school in 1963 to complete my degree requirements; Ardelia and I spent a few weeks in Trenton before summer school and lived with Raymond and his wife Barbara. It was during this time that Stephanie was conceived. I went back to school to finish my degree requirements and Ardelia went home to Eatonville.

When I went back to summer school, I did not have enough funds for room and board; I just had enough for the class that I needed. I could have stayed with my sister Sadie and her family who lived in Greensboro, but I chose to stay on campus. On the first night of school, I decided that I would "sun down" (living in rooms that you did not rent). The second and third floors of Scott Hall were not being used during the summer; all students were on the first floor. I spoke to the dean and he told me, "Just find you a room on the third floor and complete your work."

I completed my course work in the middle of August and started job hunting right away. I focused on agricultural extension, because I did not want to be confined to a classroom. The job search lasted from August to December. I went to the mail box every day looking for it to contain opportunities. While I waited, I worked with my father on the farm, marketing the tobacco, gathering corn and other matters that needed attention during and after the growing season.

Ardelia returned to Trenton after I finished my course work and the baby bump was just beginning to show. She would join me in watching for the mailman. While we were visiting with my family that winter, my father slaughtered the hogs. My mother made liver pudding and gave a small portion to me for Ardelia to fry. When I gave it to Ardelia, she insisted she was not going to cook it, because it did not look appetizing. I pleaded with her and went back outside. After a few minutes, Ardelia was at the back door whispering for me to come in the house. She wanted me to bring her more of the liver pudding because she had eaten it and said she liked it.

Beginning a Career in Monroe

The first of December 1963, I had an appointment to meet with the Agricultural Extension Agent and the Board of County Commissioners in Halifax County, North Carolina. Before that appointment could be kept, the county commissioners decided not to fill the position.

I was then told to call Mr. P. E. Bazemore in Monroe, North Carolina. They had an opening for an Assistant Agricultural Extension Agent for Union County. I called Mr. Bazemore and made an appointment to meet him and the Union County Board of Commissioners. I went to Monroe by bus and met with Mr. Bazemore for a couple of hours; then we went to a board of commissioners meeting. At this meeting, the board chair recognized Mr. Bazemore; he presented me to the board, reviewed the duties and responsibilities of the position, and recommended that I be employed as Assistant Agricultural Extension Agent for Union County. The chair asked for a motion.

The motion to approve the employment of Cecil Brown was made, seconded and approved unanimously. I had my first job! Bazemore's recommendation made the difference and I signed the necessary paperwork. I had just joined the workforce at twenty-two years of age.

On the way out of the building following the interview, I asked Mr. Bazemore about the salary. He told me it would be $5000 per year even though I was only expecting $4800. Mr. Bazemore took me to a nearby furniture store where I was given credit based solely on his recommendation. Then we went to a real estate agent and rented a two-bedroom, small, concrete block house.

My father had given me a blank signed check to buy a car if I got the job, so from there Mr. Bazemore took me to the Ford dealer. I found a car that I liked and called my father to ask, "How much do I put on the check?" He responded by saying, "Whatever you think you should." I could not decide so I called him again and I got the same response! I gave up and took the bus back to Kinston.

My father picked me up at the bus station and asked why I did not get the car. I told him I did not know how much to put down. A few days later, we went to Kinston to the Ford dealer and the same thing happened. I looked at the same car I had seen in Monroe, but he wouldn't tell me how much to put on the check. We came back home. The next day, my father came home with a 1957 Ford. He said, "Since you could not decide, I bought you that Ford out there."

I didn't realize until later that I was only the second child that he bought a car for when we finished college, even though I was the sixth born.

My dad and uncle Johnnie followed Ardelia and me to Monroe, to drop off a bedroom set and clothes. After they put up the bed, they got in the truck and headed back to Trenton. I was surprised that they just emptied the truck and left us there. I looked behind me and there was Ardelia standing there crying. In that moment, I put my arms around her, and told her that everything was going to be alright. Stephanie was due in a few weeks and I was afraid, but sometimes you must walk through the fire; with God's help, I became a man that day. I made the bed and got her in bed. With a mop that we brought with us, I mopped all the concrete floors, went to the store, got food and prepared dinner.

After everything was settled, I took a moment to pray and shed a few tears, crying because I realized that I was responsible now. Reggie Lowe would tell me that if you want your prayer to be answered you must get off your knees and when you're done, get to work. That was true then and it is true today unless the Holy Spirit tells you to sit and wait on the Lord.

My first day of work was February 1, 1964. On that first day, I was introduced to the staff which consisted of Annie Shad, secretary, and Jeanette Sherrod, Home Economics Agent. They held a meet and greet for the residents of Union County. I was surprised at the turnout that stopped by to meet me.

Many asked about Marion Odessa, my sister, who had worked in Union County as an Assistant Home Economics Agent, telling me how much they missed her. My reception and ease of meeting and working with the citizens, I know now, was because Odessa had worked there, and she left a reputation which opened so many doors of homes and farms to me. I just had to go to work. I did not have to prove myself because Odessa had already paved the way.

LIFE LESSON: It is important for children to know that one child's actions will affect the perception of others in the same family. If the bar is set low, low expectations may be expected. Odessa set the bar high.

My second day on the new job, Mr. Bazemore met with me, went over a few policies and procedures and gave me two assignments, both with dairy farmers in Waddington, NC. We went over the issues to be discussed with these farmers, but we did not discuss what outcome he would like to see.

He gave me the addresses, some general directions and then said, "When you have the opportunity to employ your own staff, hire someone who knows more then you about the subject. Give them the freedom to succeed and never smother their creativity; they will make you look good." I thought about that statement as I wondered around the county trying to find my first two farmers. In my meandering, I even ended up in South Carolina, almost to Lancaster, SC. I finally realized that when the highways change from concrete to asphalt, I was in the state of South Carolina. I eventually found the two farmers!

When Mr. Bazemore was going through the budget process, he told me he never recommended a raise for himself, because he wanted to know what the upper management thought of him, and because he wanted to set a good example for his people. He said he would write down privately what he expected, and he always received more.

During the early days of working with Mr. Bazemore, we toured the county and we discussed extension programs and the role that he had for me including 4-H, dairy farmers, and some assistance with swine and row crops. He also told me what he expected from me and he shared with me what I could expect from him.

He would provide the resources for me to do my job; he promised that if he did not do that, he would take the blame for any lack of success. He also taught me how important it is to know your product, such as the latest information on dairy farming and the dairy farmer's goals. He encouraged me to get to know the families and the expectations they had for their family and their expectations from me. He suggested that we should provide the farm families sources of up to date best practices information. Finally, he encouraged me to use him as a resource. During those days of riding through the county, I came to see and appreciate a man that loved what he was doing and who enjoyed what he was doing to improve the lives of the people of Union County.

Mr. Bazemore experienced so much discrimination! When statewide Extension Services meetings were held, black agents and home economists were invited during those early years of integration, but they had no say in planning state meetings, nor did they have any role in actively participating in the conferences. We were just allowed in the room. Blacks were called on at the end of conferences with the presiding official saying, "I see we have our colored friends here. Will you all please sing?" Only it sounded more like "sang". One agent would lead the others in an old Negro spiritual. A song would be sung, and the American social order would just roll on.

Union County had segregated office facilities; we had a small house for our office. When I moved in, my office was in the kitchen. This was the year before they integrated the extension service. After integration was the first time our team shared office space with whites, but home economic programs as well as 4-H clubs were still segregated.

When they picked new leaders after integration, Jim Morris, the white Chairman, was chosen as the chairman of the consolidated extension service. Even some white famers questioned that decision, because Bazemore was respected by all, not just in

Union County, but throughout the state. I was appointed to be the head of youth programs, including 4H. 4H clubs at one time was associated with the school system, but moved to the community which created the need for volunteer leaders. We were required to recruit and train the leader to lead their 4-H clubs. M.C. Harrell and Rachel Fowler were the other two agents. I worked with the black youth and they worked with the white youth.

We held local competitions in talent and livestock judging to determine who would represent the county in state events. After my second year with the program, the two white agents supposedly reported to me but made more money than me. At one point I had a meeting with the county budget director, who inquired as to why I was making less than the other two agents. Jim Morris's answer was that I graduated from A&T while the other two had graduated from NC State. I compared the course books and they were the same. The real reason was race. When I left, we had 50 youth clubs. The only real integration was at state and local events. I was very successful in building youth programs in Monroe, getting volunteers to work with the kids. We expanded the programs and won lots of awards. All of this was when I was only 22 years old.

As I look back over my career, Union County was one of the best employment decisions in my life because of Bazemore, who was my first supervisor; he was also my mentor and a dear friend. He had been my sister Odessa's supervisor when she worked in Union County also. The decision made by the Board of County

Commissioners in Halifax County back in December of 1963 was the decision that set me on a new path in this journey called LIFE.

LIFE LESSON: Hire smart people, provide them resources and get out of their way.

One Saturday afternoon, February 29, Ardelia wanted to go out for a ride around town. On the way home, the car stopped and would go no further. The gas gauge said 1/3 of a tank, so I said it could not be out of gas. After trying and looking for other reasons, I decided to go to a nearby station and got a two gallon can to put gas in the car. When we added gas, it started just fine.

We went to the hospital to deliver Stephanie the same night; she was born, March 1, 1964. Had we not taken that ride earlier in the day, we would have run out of gas on the way to the hospital.

Two significant families lived on the same block where we lived: Redmans and the Heaths. Patricia Redman was five or six years old and would come and see Stephanie daily. She would take her outside and sometimes to her home, which was only two houses down from our house.

During these times other federal agencies were required to hire minorities. One manager interviewed Ardelia and another black female. The other female was very light skinned, and she got the job. He later hired Ardelia as well but told her, "Don't you ever forget you're a N…." She disregarded this hateful treatment because she was focused on her goal: working to earn enough money so she could go back and finish her degree requirements at A&T. She did so in 1967 and graduated with a degree in History. She would later go on to earn a Masters' degree and become state certified as a K-12 Principal.

I stayed one more year in Monroe, commuting to Greensboro to be with the family on weekends, before I moved back to Greensboro to take a position there. Many of the relationships I formed in Monroe are still intact today. There was a young man, named Larry, from one of my 4H groups, when he retired from Duke. When he was retiring from Duke Power in Charlotte, he called to check on me. Patricia Redman is in our life today after after concluding a successful career in education.

In 1964, Congress passed The Economic Opportunity Act of 1964 which initiated President Lyndon Johnson's War on Poverty. The Federal Office of Economic Opportunity (OEO) was established as a part of that initiative. Mr. Bazemore was on a board that was established by Union County to review and make recommendations on this new federal initiative. This board created the Office of Economic Opportunity (OEO) for Anson and Union Counties. When the agency started to recruit staff, Mr. Bazemore gave me a copy of the announcement. I discussed the idea of applying and he said, "If you decide that this is something you want to do, I will give them my recommendation."

I followed his advice and applied for the position of Director of Neighborhood Youth Corps for Anson and Union County.

I was hired and my career path took a change; the winding road was just beginning. The OEO funded the Neighborhood Youth Corps as well as the Community Action Program. Bill Brock was the Director of the Anson/Union Community Action Program. Bill had two white females on his staff who worked as community organizers and a black female as his assistant. Bill later worked with the "Carolina Fund", a North Carolina program started by Governor Terry Sanford. Later in his career, Bill served as the facilitator for the Durham City/County school integration, the effort that brought together C. P. Ellis, a former Grand Dragon for the KKK, and Ann Atwater, an African American community activist.

As Director of the Neighborhood Youth Corp Program in Anson County and Union County, I was responsible for in school programs (students age 14-18) and out of school programs for drop outs (up to age 21). The original program called for the maximum enrollment of 75 in school students and 75 school dropouts.

The in-school kids were paired up with custodial employees, cafeteria workers and playground aides, and assisted teachers where needed. The Neighborhood Youth Corp paid these students to help them provide for their families; the work also gave them positive things to do. We provided an after-school remedial reading program as well as GED programs for dropouts. They worked in public service agencies, like the bus garage, recreation facilities, libraries and hospitals.

George Fuller was the Director of Operation Breakthrough in Durham. He had been invited to come to Monroe for a speaking engagement. On the afternoon of the scheduled speech, we got word there would be Ku Klux Klan activity, so we notified the sheriff. He ignored it. Instead people from the community came with guns to protect the event but the Klan didn't show up.

As the Neighborhood Youth Corps Director, I hired a secretary, a young woman named Sally. Each year, the US Department of Labor Regional Manager would give us a dollar figure and tell us to build our budget and programs based on their guidance. Sally and I had to travel to Raleigh to present our proposed budget to the federal Program Representatives.

When we were standing in line waiting to make our presentation, Sally cut the line and went straight to the front and was permitted to make our budget presentation to them without me. When she came back, she told me they had added money to our budget, enough to add fifty additional in-school students. We had to revise our program of work incorporating the additional money and she would take it back to get their approval.

When she came back to me after sharing the revised program with them, she said that we needed to go home fast. She told me, "I need to get home as quick as possible back to Monroe. It would be wasting money to stay after we had our programs approved." When we were out of the city limits of Raleigh, she told me she had agreed to have dinner with them and had made some suggestive promises to them to get those additional funds. Sally left her role in Monroe later and became the Director of the program in Gaston County.

One evening, the entire Anson-Union County staff went to a restaurant, celebrating the birthday of one of our female middle-aged white co-workers. Her son and daughter-in-law met us as we were going in the restaurant. Her son, a local Methodist Minister, walked by us without even acknowledging our presence; he only looked at his mother. She told us he didn't like her working with us, which was obvious from his behavior.

With racial tension in the air around Johnson's War on Poverty program, I decided to get a pistol. I went to the sheriff's office to get a permit and my request was refused. The sheriff said I might hurt myself. I left the sheriff's office and went to the hardware store and purchased a twenty-two-pump-action rifle. I would sleep with the rifle by the bed until I left Monroe for Greensboro.

Mr. Bazemore was the lead plaintiff in *Bazemore v. Friday* class action suit against state and local officials in federal court alleging discrimination in employment and failure to eliminate salary disparities between white and black extension employees and in the provision of services through the Extension Service.

The case was originally filed in 1971; it went all the way to the US Supreme Court and was finally decided in favor of the *Bazemore* plaintiffs on demand from the Supreme Court to the US Court of Appeals, Fourth Circuit in 1988. Mr. Bazemore never wavered. He saw this suit to its conclusion.

When Mr. Bazemore passed. I attended his funeral in Monroe. The church was filled with not just citizens from Union County and Monroe but citizens that he had been involved with from across the state. The comments that were shared in the crowd after the funeral outside the church made me further realize how blessed I was to have had the opportunity to learn from him and to be mentored by him.

I started drinking regularly while living in Monroe. After I left the extension service, Ardelia had gone back to school at A&T in 1967 and took Stephanie with her to live in an apartment in Greensboro, so I was home alone most weekdays. I got to a point where I had a drink every day after a "hard" day's work. I thought I "deserved" a drink, which was a big mistake and became a dangerous pattern.

During this time, there were demonstrations on A&T's campus. The apartment we had in Greensboro was a few blocks from campus and faced Memorial Coliseum on Lindsey Street. We woke up one morning to National Guard helicopters overhead and tear gas filling the air; they were firing on demonstrators. Windows were shot out in Scott Hall, the men's dormitory on

A&T's campus. Bullet marks were on the face of Scott Hall for many years and were a continual reminder of that day that a student, Willie Grimes was killed fighting for justice. The bullet marks only disappeared when Scott Hall was torn down and replaced with a new student housing complex composed of four pods; each pod is named after one of the Greensboro four: Blair, Bell, McNeil and McCain.

Greensboro and Guilford County Directorship

After a few years in Monroe, I moved to Greensboro to work as Director for the OEO Neighborhood Youth Corps of Guilford County in 1968. The Guilford County program had three to four times the number of youth participants of Anson and Union Counties. The program also had considerably more money and was engaged with more community resources than Anson and Union Counties.

During a reception on my first day of work, I met a young man by the name of Michael James. We talked at length about our background and the issues facing Greensboro and Guilford County. I also met Don Forney, the Assistant Director of the Guilford County Community Action Program, who was stationed in the High Point office.

Michael was a community organizer with his hand on the pulse of the City and the low-income community. I solicited his help in identifying young people that met the criteria to become enrollees in the in-school and out of school programs which I was responsible for managing. Michael also helped me by connecting me with many people of influence in the African American community.

I was never one to sit behind a desk if I did not have to. I would visit the neighborhood center to seek and encourage the staff. I would also encourage youth to apply to our program. Those applications would come into my office, where my staff would follow up and place as many of the youth as the program allowed. At that time, a prevalent thought among youth program leadership was that if the United States government really wanted to address youth issues, they should require mandatory military service for young men.

Jason McCall was a young man in our programs in Greensboro. He enlisted in the Army at the age of seventeen and was sent to Fort Jackson. A little while later, his grandmother asked me to help him get out. I spoke to his commanding officer and he said he will be fine. A few months later, he was in my office in a uniform, smiling and doing well. Military service deeply impacts a young man, usually for the better. It gets them off the streets, teaches them discipline and gives them purpose. And in most cases, it gives them a skill that is transferable to private life.

I would also visit Don's office in High Point promoting the youth program. My contact with Don was initially more of a passing relationship, including little program talks and whatever the flavor of the day may be. When I was in Greensboro and later in High Point, I would spend a considerable amount of time talking to various staff and people connected in the community. Bazemore's counsel from my time in Monroe shaped my management thinking for the rest of my life. I built a good program and staff as a result.

Paul Gazon was the OEO Director in Guilford County and left in 1967. When the hiring process started, a Guilford County OEO board member suggested considering hiring a black Director. Another board member responded that no blacks in North Carolina were qualified to fill Gazon's position and insisted we would have to go to New York or Baltimore to find someone black that was qualified. In the same meeting, Mary Ross, a white female, spoke out against that statement; she was the director of a young adult work study program. Her clout was connected to her husband, who was a prominent citizen in the community.

The next morning Mary was in my office expressing how she could not believe the racism against me and how crazy some people are. I was invited to a meeting a few days later with a few black board members and black community organizers, as well as Dr. George Simpkins, the Chairman of the local chapter of the NAACP. The discussion focused on me; they wanted to determine my desire and willingness to fill Gazon's position, to be the next Director of the Agency.

Austin Davis was a field representative for the US Department of Labor and was in favor of me for the position. My relationships with Michael James and his wife and with Don Forney became a supportive arm which solidified as they fought to have me become the next Director. The board was divided along racial lines; African American board members wanted me but didn't have the votes.

One morning, two board members called and invited me to have dinner with them at the Jumping Run Clubhouse later that week. I agreed. Later the same day, I stopped by the Community Center and spoke with Michael about that invitation to dinner. He told me that there was a community meeting being planned at the community center the same evening and he would love for me to stop by and give some remarks about my desire to serve the community as the Director of the Agency. I indicated I might be a little late since they were going to pick me up from home.

When the board members picked me up, I told them that I needed to stop by the Community Center to make some remarks to the residences about the Neighborhood Youth Corp. When we drove up to the Center it was clear that the place was crowded; the parking lot was overflowing with cars. We got out of the car and as soon as we entered the gym, the crowd started calling my name.

Michael quieted the crowd and introduced me. I made a few remarks and received a standing ovation from the crowd. When we got in the car, one of the board members said, "You have too much power; there is no need for us to have dinner." They immediately took me back home. They never explained their intentions, but I think they were hoping to talk me into publicly rejecting the position, so they could quiet the unrest among the community. At the Community Center rally, they realized their hopes were futile.

A few days later, they offered the position to a white candidate from Connecticut. Simpkins told me I should not be at the press conference when they announced and introduced the new director. At the press conference, the newly named director thanked them for the offer of the position and then declined to accept it. He saw the unrest in the community and knew the volatility surrounding the agency; he didn't want to be a part of it.

I watched the press conference on noon news on TV from a motel room, where I was holding up at Simpkins' suggestion. Over the next few days, they said they were willing to hire a black person, but they were determined to get me out of Greensboro. The Board hired Jerome Black, a retired principal from South Carolina.

Electronics Program

Shortly thereafter the Board assigned me as Director of an OEO vocational training program for teenagers which had an electronics training component, partnered with a training school business. The school leadership had told a black employee from New York that he was coming to Greensboro to serve as the school's Director, but they made him my assistant instead, after pressure from the Board.

I hired George Roper as a program director; he was a retired military man who knew electronics. We needed to order TVs for the programs so that we could use them for instructional purposes to train students in electronics servicing and repair. The purchase order was sent to the local partner for the training school business.

After about two weeks, a U-Haul truck showed up with TVs. I was in the process of signing the delivery order, but before I could, George took the form out of my hands and insisted on inspecting the inventory in the van. We had ordered new TVs and there were no new TVs on the truck. They had sent a truck load of old, used TVs that had obviously been part of a hotel or motel inventory.

We told the driver to take them back. The driver called the partner and he was more than upset with me. Mr. Roper and I went back in the building and left the driver in the parking lot. After a few minutes, he drove off.

A few weeks later, we received half our order, but never received what the grant agreement required. I authorized payment for only the items received. I never received any push back on that decision.

We were having all these problems trying to move forward and serve the students, so I decided to call the federal agency in Washington, DC about our issues in Greensboro. The local program managers wanted me to use cash instead of checks to pay student enrollees, creating another opportunity for mistakes and theft.

I was left with only one choice. I notified the DC office of the procedure: each withdrawal, I would take an employee with me and would count the money. I would make a written note, copy it for the office file, for my personal file and for the DC central office. Local leadership did not know that I was maintaining a log on everything I deemed inappropriate and reporting it to the federal office in Washington DC.

One day, one of the partners called and said they wanted us to go to Washington to explain the problems that were coming up in the program. Secretly, he was trying to get me out of the way, so he could elevate his own man as the Director, so they could change the program content and cost sharing. They also hoped to pin the blame for the issues on me because I was not cooperating with them or falling in line.

I left that morning for DC, knowing I was in a trap because he was blaming me for what he said was a misappropriation of funds. Amy Reed, the chief administrator for the federal funding office was aware of all the items because I had sent them to her. When we met in person, she realized that she knew my family from back home in Trenton, North Carolina.

During a break, Ms. Reed spoke to me in private and asked me if I was from Trenton and if I had a brother named Robert. She said, "I am James's sister." James had been on the 1958 basketball team that fought in Scott Hall after our first win in the state playoffs and lost the next day. She thanked me for sending the material that I had been sending to her office. Ms. Reed recognized what was going on in the program and that they were trying to blame me for the audit irregularities. Ultimately, she held them accountable.

When we boarded the plane, the partner did not speak to me on the flight back to Greensboro. The federal agency contracted with a national audit firm to audit the books. Once the audit was completed, the training school owners were required to reimburse the federal government in an amount that exceeded six figures, and my record keeping was a factor of getting to the truth.

We lived in Greensboro on a block with a minister and his wife, a school teacher, an assistant athletic director, three IBM employees and the dean of students for A&T. I became part-time drinking buddies with one of them.

On the home front, Stephanie was in kindergarten at a Catholic school. One day, I sent my friend Martin to pick her up from kindergarten, as she was supposed to be picked up each day at 1pm. Martin didn't go! When I realized she was still at the school, I went ballistic. I went to the school at 4pm and found Stephanie standing by a tree, crying because everyone else had gone home, and she was alone and afraid.

LIFE LESSON: Do not give responsibilities to unreliable people.

Stephanie stayed in Catholic school until 6th grade. She went to Junior High at Aycock Junior High in Greensboro, N.C. and did her first year of high school in Shreveport, Louisiana.

On March 23, 1974, North Carolina State played UCLA in the NCAA national finals game. State was coached by Norm Sloan and that team roster included State legends David Thompson, Tom Burleson and Monty Towe. State beat UCLA 80-77 in double overtime, ending UCLA's seven-year run of NCAA national titles. By the end of the game, my drinking buddy and I were laid out on my floor from drinking.

High Point

Cecil Brown

I received a call from Don Forney in 1970, who was now Director of the High Point Model Cities program. Model Cities was a HUD initiative designed to experiment with new strategies in pilot areas to improve on HUD's previous work with the Urban Renewal program to serve low income communities.

Urban Renewal had focused on physical factors like building and relocation, while Model Cities was working to add a human services component. Don presented me with a potential new opportunity with this program. Dr. Simpkins from the Greensboro NAACP encouraged me to take this job.

Don J. Forney was a black man in North Carolina before his time. I say that because he made key connections that could cause the establishment to move. He told me he understood what I wanted to accomplish in Greensboro, but he did not think the fight would be worth it. He knew the powerful board members would do all they could to make my life hell. He suggested that you never want to be in a position this day and age when all the noise will be about you. You must protect yourself because you may be damaging your long-term future if you do.

After a lengthy discussion, I agreed that for the good of the Greensboro Community Action Program and to be involved in a program that, if successful, would have a major impact on low income communities across this country, I would accept the Model Cities job as Director of Information and Evaluation services.

The challenge of this position was to develop an evaluation tool that could be used to evaluate the impact of the model city and its components on the low-income communities. The identified strengths could be transferred to the Community Development

Block Grant Program, which was working to serve communities across the country.

Don asked me what I thought the outcome should look like for the overall program. My response was, "to improve the quality of life of the citizens affected by the programs, both physical and the individual sense of well-being." Don then asked whether I thought I could collect that kind of information. I assured him that I could by collecting information from the recipients of the programs. Only they would know if their quality of life had improved as a result of the program's interventions in their lives. He asked when I could start.

When Don hired me to work in the Model Cities program, he told me to build the program and to take the responsibility. He would be available for counsel, but it would be my call unless I violated a federal rule. He was a manager that deflected any praise for himself and gave the accolades to his staff. He was known to say that his only asset was the ability to find good, intelligent people. I think that may have been a subtle jab to non-blacks because his staff was at least ninety-five percent black.

Don was the first black person with his own television show in the region; it aired on the local High Point station channel 8 on Sunday mornings. The show was about community issues, and it served as a platform for him to get the community to talk about issues that may not otherwise have been part of the public discussion. Don was also a business man; he owned a night club in Greensboro which he operated until his death.

The initial staff of the Information and Evaluation Section consisted of Rosetta James, Linda Murry and me. Rosetta had worked for the school system in High Point and Linda had worked in the High Point office of the Greensboro OEO. My first meeting with the two staff members was designed to share who we were as individuals and to find out everyone's strengths, weaknesses, and beliefs. After a day of talking, I realized that this team had a perfect chemistry. I was the big picture, idea and planning type and Linda was a strong internal organizer with a love for disadvantaged people; Rosetta was both a vital information source on the High Point disadvantaged community and a lady with the courage and desire to make positive changes in her community.

Before we ended our first day, we decided that we would build our evaluation around High Point's Urban Renewal program. The Urban Renewal Program was to be replaced by the Community Development Block Grant Programs and rolled out across the United States based on insights gained from the Model Cities program.

We started the design by identifying the conditions that existed in the urban renewal area and the activities undertaken by the Urban Renewal programs to bring about change in the physical and human environment. We also identified the quality issues reported by the citizens that had been impacted by the programs.

Our design for data collection included input measures such as dollar amount, staff cost, and all other overhead costs. We also included the number of houses rehabbed and associated cost, as well as street improvement and brick and mortar costs. For the residents, we wanted to know the direct impacts, both positive and negative, and we wanted to document overall impact, positive and negative, on the quality of life of residents.

Our urban renewal evaluation demonstrated that from a quality of life perspective the program was a total failure, because it destroyed the social network that residents had relied on for years. We had residents telling us that their friends were no longer together. It is discouraging when you hear things like: *"my house is better, but now I cannot get to church because the person that took me to church lives in another community." "we live in a better house, but I don't have that neighbor who was a life line." "The guy who used to pick me up and take me to church or the grocery store isn't available now because the program moved him across town." "It's great that I'm in a better house but if I can't get to help and none of my friends are close, it's not great anymore."* We realized that the Urban Renewal programs had no real emphasis on quality of life issues. These had been completely left out of the program.

There were three Model Cities in North Carolina: Asheville, Winston-Salem and High Point. Each city established an information and evaluation team which designed its own evaluation system. Part of the evaluation program was to determine what worked and what didn't.

At the end of eighteen months, the evaluation staffs of the three cities met in Asheville to finalize the plan to measure the results of Model Cities impact. After a day of blending each city model, we submitted a final report and recommended the model to the Department of Housing and Urban Development.

We concluded there was more human success from social programs and less impact from housing improvements because they took longer to measure results. The information we collected in the Model Cities pilots set the stage for the subsequent Community Development Block Grant program. The launches across the country included a large human services component. We recognized that the innovative programs we needed to plan for Model Cities must consider the adverse impact of destroying the social network of affected residents.

One of the first Model Cities projects that we evaluated was the cardiovascular catheterization Lab, which had been built in High Point. There were major questions as to its impact on disadvantaged citizens. First, we conducted an in-house analysis and looked at both the inputs and outputs measured by the program. Then we entered into an operational agreement and met with the Hospital Administration to conduct more analysis. We concluded by reconciling the results from all the analysis. The first-year results indicated that a substantial portion of beneficiaries of the Lab were low income residents living in the Model Cities community and their quality of life had improved as a result of the Lab.

When the Model Cities experiment was completed, the program was merged into other HUD programming and the City of High Point took over the administrative functions; my division, Information and Evaluation, was the only function that was transferred to the City of High Point Department of Community Development. My position became Director of Information and Evaluation and I had an increase in the number of staffs allocated to the division.

While working for the City of High Point, I attended an annual conference of the International City Manager Association in Montreal, Canada. Three city staff members attended, two white and me. As we were clearing customs, I was pulled out of line and taken into a room on the Canadian side. My traveling partners looked back and then kept walking.

An agent came in, looked at my papers, and asked if the documents were in my real name. "Yes," I responded. "Have you ever used another name?" "No". He left the room and a half hour passed; then another man walked in with a question, "Have you ever lived in Canada or is this your first time here?" "I have never lived here, and this is my first time."

He left the room and another hour passed; they came back and told me I was free to go. I picked up my bags and went out into the terminal looking for my co-workers. They were nowhere to be found, so I caught a cab to the hotel. When I walked in, the two of them had changed into their tennis shorts and white tennis shoes and were heading to the tennis court with rackets. They said, "See, you made it!" and kept walking. They never asked me what the agents had wanted; it didn't surprise or even seem to matter to them that I had been detained or treated that way.

In my public service career, I have seen and been an unwilling participant in blatant racial discrimination. Once I was attending a meeting of the NC League of Cities and was standing with two white co-workers, making small talk. High Point's Mayor came up to me and asked me to come with him. I followed him across the room, and he introduced me to the Mayor of Charlotte by saying, "See, we got us one." The Charlotte Mayor looked at me in shock that my Mayor had been so callous to my face. He shook my hand and I went outside to catch my breath.

After a year as the Director of Community Development, my department head moved to Clearwater, Florida, and I was appointed to his role, which made me the first black department head in High Point local government history. I later applied for the position of Assistant City Manager. When I approached the current City Manager, David Johnson, and indicated my interest for the Assistant City Manager's position, he told me that I could better serve the City in my Development position. At the time, I felt like he was blocking me from a promotion by basically telling me not to apply.

I continued serving in that position for three years and managed a spotless program. We never had a violation finding by the Department of Housing and Urban Development during my tenure. My last monitoring letter before I left High Point consisted of a single paragraph of praise for the program administration, management and outcomes.

Shreveport, Louisiana

In 1979, I received a call from an International City/County Management Association (ICMA) minority recruiter telling me that Shreveport was looking for a Director of Urban Development; they wanted my approval to refer my name to them, which I gave. Subsequently, I received a call from the mayor of Shreveport inviting me to the city for an interview.

The afternoon before my morning interview, I arrived in Shreveport and checked in at the hotel that the city had reserved for me. Within minutes, I took a long stiff drink and went to bed thinking about the interview the next day.

The following morning, I was picked up by one of the mayor's assistants. After a lengthy interview by the mayor and some of his key staff members, we adjourned for lunch where members of the city council joined us along with other department directors.

After lunch, we had a tour of the city with emphasis on the slum and blighted communities.

In comparison at that time, High Point was receiving around $1.5 million per year of Community Development Block Grant entitlement dollars; Shreveport was receiving around $6 million per year. After the day long interview, a member of the city council took me to the airport for my flight home. Once he left the airport waiting room, I hurriedly got myself a drink, because the shakes were about to take over. As I drank the alcohol, I could feel the effect of the drink moving into every cell in my body. I know now that at that time alcohol had taken control of my life.

A few days after I returned from Shreveport, I received a call from the mayor's office that I was being offered the job as Director of Urban Development for the City of Shreveport. After discussing the offer with Ardelia, we decided to take the job. I knew whether she said so or not, that she didn't want to leave Greensboro. She agreed but only because it was what I wanted.

During this time, I was walking deeper into the valley of alcohol. I resigned my position as Director of Community Development in High Point and began to make way for a smooth transition for the department. Two farewell parties were held in my honor at City Hall; the entire High Point community was invited to attend. The night before I was to leave, my old staff held, as they put it, "a crying party", at the home of one of the employees. I went to the party, had a few drinks and left.

Before I left for Shreveport, I took a trip home to Trenton to say goodbye to my parents. Before I returned to Greensboro at the end of my visit, the last thing my mother said to me was, "I do not know anything about the place that you are going; whatever you do, TAKE GOD with you".

As I approached Salisbury, NC on my drive south, I began to feel the shakes coming over me, so I stopped and got a six pack of beer which I nursed to Tuscaloosa, Alabama. I located the hotel where I was to spend the night, checked in and asked the clerk where I could get a drink. They gave me directions to where I could get a bottle. I took that pint of liquor to my room, took a large drink, and went to sleep. I had to stay on schedule because I had a meeting scheduled with the mayor of Shreveport that Saturday morning and it was now Thursday afternoon.

On Friday morning, I got on I-20 West and continued driving in a rain storm. I drove into Shreveport late that afternoon, found the place where the city had rented a small apartment for me while I looked for a residence for me and the family. As I stood in that apartment window, looking at the city, with storm clouds rolling and a tornado warning being broadcast, I began to wonder, "What have I gotten myself into?"

I did not go to God my Creator; I went to my god in a bottle and slept until early Saturday morning. I got up and dressed for my meeting with the Mayor. As I drove to the mayor's office, I was a little apprehensive about what was to come. What new experiences and expectations would I be confronted with?

During the meeting, the mayor spoke about the city and the difficulty of changing the culture from the commission form of local government to a strong mayoral form of government. As a department head, I would report directly to the mayor. He pointed out to me that the Department of Urban Development had some challenges; the first was to respond to a monitoring letter from the US Department of Housing and Urban Development.

I left his office and went to my office. Sitting down at my desk on that Saturday morning, I noticed a brown envelope on the desk with my name on it with the word CONFIDENTIAL. Upon opening the envelope, I noticed that it was from HUD. It was the monitoring letter that the mayor had just spoken to me about. I had left High Point, North Carolina where our program's monitoring letter was only one paragraph, which included the words, "outstanding program performance".

The monitoring letter for the Shreveport program was thirteen pages long, with the final kicker in the letter saying that if the city failed to have a minimum of $10 million under contract by December 31, 1979, the city would lose its entitlement of $6.5

million. I laid my head on the desk and again said, "Lord, what have I gotten myself into? Help me!"

I went back to my little one room apartment, made some lunch, sat at the ninth-story window and read the letter again. I read it issue by issue and drafted viable solutions that I felt would give the department a chance to meet the $10.5 million goal. A monumental task, but it felt like it might be attainable.

I decided not to talk to the staff about the situation as a group because the lack of progress was clearly, in part, due to performance issues. I could tell it was also due to a lack of leadership and the change in the form of government.

I decided that the first order of business on my first Monday morning as the Director of Urban Development would be simply to introduce myself to the staff as a group, lay out my expectations for the department and the staff, and what they could expect from me. Then I held one-hour meetings with individual members of the team. My plan for the order of the individual meetings was with the current assistant director being last and the administrative clerk being first.

LIFE LESSON: My belief is that you get the truth on how an organization operates by starting with the person that answers the phone and the janitor if there is one. These individuals tend to be "invisible" to many of the other employees and have insights that no one else will recognize.

After meeting with the employees, I determined that three of the employees were not a good match for the positions that they were assigned to and would be asked to be reassigned or resign. (Two resigned and I terminated the other after my first two weeks on the job.) I also decided that I was going to keep the assistant director close to me because of his political connections to the mayor and his campaign; he had close ties to the larger Shreveport community. I was also convinced that they needed a relocation division (I moved employees over to start that department) and that they needed a professional planner.

I then called the Regional HUD Director and set up an appointment to meet with him and the field representative assigned to monitor our office. The purpose of the meeting was to get HUD's perspective on the problems in Shreveport and their thoughts on the staff members that they were interacting with and to lay out my plans for meeting the December 31 deadline of encumbering $10 million in block grant funds. That was a full day. I needed a drink!

As I finished my take home dinner at the end of my first day, I took a drink and begin to develop a detailed work plan for the next thirty days. I knew I would need to really get a good plan with the necessary human resources in place to meet the December 31 deadline. The first order was to recruit and employ an urban planner as soon as possible.

By the end of the first week, the mayor's office had made plans for Ardelia and our two children to fly down so that we could look for a home and check out the schools. Stephanie would be entering high school and Michael would be entering as a first grader since he was to turn six years old on December 30th. Stephanie had been looking forward to entering Page High School in Greensboro. I was now pulling her away from her friends and from the school that she had dreamed of attending for years.

The city put my family up in a hotel and we toured the city and neighborhoods. Ardelia, Stephanie and Michael had no interest in their new home, because they were not really interested in making Shreveport their home. We found a house near Huntington High School and decided to make an offer to purchase it. The family then flew back to Greensboro.

On Monday, I went to the realtor to speak about the house and was told that Pat Lewis, wide receiver for the then St Louis Cardinals, had just paid cash for the house. The realtor said that I may want to look in the Huntington subdivision instead. That afternoon, I was leaving a meeting with the mayor and he asked me how I was doing finding housing.

When I told him, he told me to check in the original neighborhood to see if I could find another house that I might like. I told him that I had already picked out one and I was now looking for a bank to talk with to get approval. He picked up the phone and called the president of the bank where he was a former board chair. He told the bank president to have one of his loan officers call me and schedule an appointment for me to buy the house. The mayor gave him the price of the house.

I had a meeting with the bank two days later and when I arrived the loan officer and a real estate agent were in the conference room with the papers drawn up. After I gave them a check for five thousand dollars and signed the paperwork, I had a home to move the family to Shreveport.

Less than a month later, I flew home to help pack the family for the move. On the day we left for Shreveport, we packed the Pinto wagon with clothes and snacks to eat on the long drive. I rented a trailer to transport our luggage and a large plant.

The trip was uneventful until we were in the State of Mississippi. Around four o'clock in the afternoon, my car just stopped running. I pulled off to the side of the road and said to myself, "My God, not in Mississippi."

Just the idea of this happening in Mississippi raised uneasiness in me. Not in Mississippi! After about ten minutes of waiting, a State Trooper pulled up behind me. It was a welcome sight, but I was still anxious because it was Mississippi.

Fear of all the ugliest impressions of Mississippi showered down on me. The trooper walked up to my window and asked what was the problem. I told him, "My car just stopped." He called for a tow truck and said, "I will stay here with you until the tow truck arrives."

Once the tow truck arrived, he told the tow truck driver to take the car to the Ford dealer in Jackson. He told me to ride with the tow truck driver and my family would ride with him. We left for Jackson and my mind is still racing. Emmett Till, Medgar Evers, Goodman and Chaney, the KKK; all of this is running through my mind.

We pulled in to the service area at the Ford dealer. The trooper got out and said to the manager of the shop, "Got here a man and his family on their way to Shreveport. Can you help him?" The shop was in the process of closing for the day.

The manager asked if anyone would be willing to stay and see if they could get me back on the road. Three mechanics volunteered to repair my car. The trooper thanked the mechanics and he wished us well. I thanked him and said good night to him.

As he drove off, there was my family and three white men in greasy coveralls. My family and I took a seat in the lounge. After about forty-five minutes, a mechanic announced that we were ready to go. They hooked the trailer to the car; I paid the bill and we were on our way. We arrived in Shreveport to our new home in the wee hours of the morning. Mississippi was good to us that day.

LIFE LESSON: Do not judge.

To secure the services of a good urban planner, I sat down with the Director of Human Resources for the city, only to find that the system of securing personnel was a "good old boy system" where department heads employed their friends and friends of friends. I was told, "Find someone that you know that will do the job that you need to get done."

Later that day I reached out to John Bryant, a friend that I had worked with in Greensboro as a planner for several years. He had a masters' degree in Urban and Regional Planning. We invited him to the city, where he was interviewed by the Human Resources Director and the mayor.

I wanted them to interview John to confirm my belief that he was a good fit for our needs. They were both impressed with his educational background and his work history. The mayor told me to make him an offer if he was my choice to help meet the challenges facing the department. After two hours, John came to me with his impressions which were very much in line with what I had written a few days before. I told him that I would be sending an offer letter. Considering the obstacles and challenges before the department, I wanted him to consider all factors.

Later that day, I received a return call from Jason James, Field Office Director of HUD for the region. We agreed that I would fly to New Orleans two days later to meet with the central office staff, the Field Representative for Shreveport and Mr. James. During that meeting, it was decided that the field representative would visit Shreveport in one month to check on our progress in responding to the monitoring letter issues.

When I returned to Shreveport, I called my assistant director and my budget director into my office and had them bring all the project files. We discussed all the major elements of each project and identified resource needs for each. The budget director was to set up a financial management system for each project and the assistant director would identify all the human resources that would be needed. If we did not have the personnel on staff, he should identify what skills were needed, like relocation housing and engineering services. He should also collect company names and information on the city's history with these firms. I committed myself to draft bid packages for all projects that required engineering services.

Over the next two days, all bid packages were typed and made ready to be mailed out to potential bidders. The two directors completed their tasks and we were ready to package things up and go to City Council. I took the packages to the mayor's office for his staff review, and I ran into the mayor in the hallway. I explained why I was there, and he invited me into his office.

He looked through all the bids, circling the estimated project cost with a red marker. He then picked up the phone and called his campaign manager and asked for the engineering firms that had donated to his election campaign. Upon receiving this information, he assigned projects to firms, I think according to their campaign contribution. He then told me to call these companies and let them know about the project and that the city attorney would be preparing the necessary contracts. I was to have the contracts ready for the city council to approve in two weeks and then ready for the firms to sign.

Having just left a local government in North Carolina, I was completely dumbfounded by this action. In North Carolina, bidding was always required for projects over a specific dollar amount.

I went back to the office and called Councilman Greg Wall, a black councilman. I went to his office and shared this with him, then asked him what I should do. He looked at me and said, "Boy, you can get a BS in political science in North Carolina in four years and you can get a Bachelor's and Master's degree in Political Science in Louisiana in one year!"

The mayor's office called a conference call with the mayor and other council members. The mayor told them about our meeting and what I would be bringing to council in two weeks and that he needed a majority vote.

During that call, I witnessed how things got done in Shreveport. Deals were traded and made on the call, not in public council meetings. Decisions were made to approve all the engineering contracts exactly as had been requested. I was completely blown away.

Councilman Wall told me that whenever I had items that were going to Council, I should sit down with him. He also told me to get to know the City Council's auditor.

After watching a few council meetings, I realized that the President of the Council and the council majority took their voting queues from the internal auditor. He was their fiscal gatekeeper.

For the remainder of my time in Shreveport, getting things through Council was easy. For all my agenda items, I would sit down with the internal auditor, or one of his staff members, and then meet with Councilman Wall; he in turn would call key council members for a quick conference call to discuss items. Sometimes vote trading would take place in the council session.

There was one council meeting where I had over ten items that needed council approval before the project could move forward. The council process required a first and second reading on financial matters before passing. At this meeting, the council suspended the rules and then proceeded to approve all ten items on first reading by unanimous vote. Other department heads could not understand how that happened and I never told.

An editorial appeared in one of the regional newspapers concerning the staff that the mayor had assembled by employing department directors from outside the State of Louisiana. To show the newspaper's true colors, they used cartoon characters of animals to represent each department director along with the salary. The animal used to represent me was that of a raccoon, hanging on a tree limb by the tail, with black rim glasses and my salary of $29,900. ***Welcome to Shreveport!***

During that time in Shreveport, my addiction was continuing its progression. I couldn't brush my teeth without taking a drink! I realize now that I was attempting to run from myself by going to Shreveport. Belatedly, I realized that you can't run from yourself; if you're there, the unfamiliar places will feel the same. Alcoholism is so powerful, you think you're okay and nobody knows but you, but everyone around you knows.

On the family front, Michael wouldn't have been in school if we had stayed in Greensboro, however the school cutoff dates in Shreveport were later so he could start at five. Every afternoon in Shreveport, Michael would be sitting on the curb when I came home from work with his Steelers helmet and Terry Bradshaw jersey, waiting to play football. He did not have friends in the neighborhood his age, so I became his center and wide receiver.

Stephanie started high school at Huntington High; she made a few friends, but it wasn't Page High. When we left Greensboro, Ardelia had been teaching full time. However, she didn't meet all the Caddo Parish teacher requirements, so she was employed as a full-time substitute. The family had a strong dislike for Shreveport for these reasons, as well as my drinking every afternoon.

In North Carolina, you don't accept gifts from contractors. Shreveport was different, but I didn't take any of the offers. I just could not accept quid pro quos.

A contractor was cutting trees and offered me firewood. I rejected it, but he delivered two 20ft racks of firewood, along with two smoked turkeys. When I arrived and saw the firewood, I called and told him to come and pick up the wood and the turkeys. It was all picked up the next morning before I went to work.

The first or second week after arriving in Shreveport I was invited to a community meeting in the community development target area. The rental properties were in such deplorable condition that people were withholding their rent payments. I was asked by a council member and the mayor to see what we could do to make things better. We went to the meeting with several staff and council members. Residents attacked the other new department heads and me as an outsider, saying there was no way we could help. Some attacked the mayor for hiring staff that "did not know a thing about Shreveport."

I invited three of the residents, Mrs. Walley, Mrs. Goins and Mrs. Franklin, to meet over lunch at a local restaurant. After they saw what I had to offer, they told me I had their support and that they would be available to speak for us when needed. These residents opened doors in the community that would have taken me a very long time to open. We were able to relocate a few residents, but not solve all the problems.

Neighborhood Housing Services (NHS) was funded by the department I was responsible for. I had a problem with the way NHS was spending its funding. They wanted to build; I thought they should rehab property including rental property. This became an issue between the Director of the NHS and me.

I spoke to the mayor and he appointed me to the NHS board and along with the three neighborhood activists, we changed the program. We established procedures where block grant funds were used to assist in rehabilitating rental properties with strong conditions attached. As noted previously, Councilman Wall was my ally on city council. In my regular communications with Wall, I received his help to reallocate budget funds from public works issues to housing rehabilitation.

During my first month on the new job, I spent one weekend in the hospital, trying to stop drinking and was successful for three days. But then my heart started fluttering. My cardiac system didn't do well while trying to detox. While sleeping, sometimes I would feel a kick in the chest, waking me up when I was asleep in bed with my pulse racing and misfiring. I never sought any other help while I was in Shreveport.

The mayor's chief of staff said to me that one of his staff members said they didn't think I was going to make it because of my drinking. He said he told her that everybody drinks around here. Alcohol was everywhere in Louisiana; it made drinking so easy. You could buy mixed drinks in supermarkets.

In December 1979, I walked over to the mayor's Christmas party held in a large conference room in City Hall. A staff member walked in with a gallon of booze under each arm. I said, "You can't do that; this is City Hall." His response: "THIS is Louisiana".

It was also around this time that I realized I did not like the strong mayoral form of government. Everyone worked for the mayor, so all department heads had to campaign for him. If I had stayed much longer than I did, I would have had to look for a job because the mayor lost in the next election.

When an expressway goes through urban areas, it goes through poor communities. The federal government claims it helps with urban renewal, but it's really the path of least resistance. When I went to Shreveport, there was an East-West interstate, I-20 west to California. My department was responsible for overseeing the relocation and mitigation plans for a new North-South expressway. The route for the expressway was already set when I arrived.

I went to a meeting with the Federal Highway Administration officials and they told me what properties they were planning to buy. I saw quickly to state that the people who lived in the impacted areas did not own the properties; they were renting from wealthy landlords. The owners would get a big check from the FHA and the poor people would be displaced to other poor neighborhoods, if they could find anything at all. There was not a lot of decent housing available for the people who had to move.

Another challenging point for me was the plan outlined for dealing with sub-standard housing not in but along the right of way. The federal government plan was to paint the houses one block deep along the path of the freeway as it passed through Shreveport. I raised hell on this point because they were not helping the residents, just putting a clean face on a dilapidated neighborhood. We convinced them to renovate the owner-occupied units instead and to push the owners of the remaining properties to address their substandard conditions.

I left before a final relocation plan was finalized. My last meeting with Federal Highway Administration officials on the plan was a Friday afternoon in Baton Rouge. I told them it was my last meeting, but I didn't tell them why. I flew out Saturday morning to start work as the Director of Community Development in Durham, N.C. on Monday, April 1, 1980.

Durham

I had received a call from a minority recruiter sometime earlier informing me about a position in Durham, North Carolina. He had asked if I would mind if he submitted my information to the Durham City Manager. The City Manager called me a few weeks later and asked to come visit me in Shreveport, and I agreed. I met with the manager and a few days later he called to offer me the Durham job. I flew up and met the staff, and then went back and talked to Ardelia, Stephanie and Michael. We agreed to move. I decided then that this would be our last move until both Stephanie and Michael finished high school to spare them the pain of any further transition.

When I arrived in Durham that Saturday, I checked into a hotel in downtown Durham and went downstairs to the dining room. I ran into the same federal highway administrators that I had met with the day before when I had left Baton Rouge. They were there because the Federal Highway Administration was also involved in building an east-west expressway through Durham, what is now Highway NC 147.

Crest Street neighborhood owners, with help from Legal Aid, were blocking the expressway so it would not destroy their neighborhood. I saw what a community can do if they stand up. The owners finally agreed to relocate with the condition that the developers had to rebuild all new housing to replace their small community. This requirement became part of the final relocation plan for the Crest Street community.

I was hired in Durham as the Director for Community Development. When I arrived in Durham, a council member said, "When you want things from Washington, call me and we will go see a guy I know." He never told me who this "guy" was. Later I called in this favor because we were trying to get funds for a grant that was stuck in Washington. I called the council person and we went to a big house in an upscale community in North Durham.

We sat with a middle-aged man and the council person asked me to explain the situation. After I finished, the man picked up the phone and called the congressman that represented Durham. Within ten minutes, "this guy" called us back and said he had called the office in Washington and asked a staff member, "Do you have any pens over there?" He said if they didn't, he would be happy to send some over so they could sign off on the grant application. Three days later I got a call that the funds were on the way. I still don't know who the "mystery man" of influence was.

LIFE LESSON: I have seen that it makes a difference who you talk to when you want to get things done.

Shortly after my arrival in Durham we sold our house in Shreveport and I flew to Shreveport to drive the family back to Durham. We hired movers to bring our belongings to Durham. On our trip back, I drove to Jackson, Mississippi and then Ardelia asked to drive. I got in the back seat with Michael and Stephanie moved to the front seat and I went to sleep.

When I woke up, we were north of Atlanta, headed to North Carolina. I started driving again around Charlotte and I pulled off I-85 in Durham, on to Highway NC 751 in a wooded area. The family had not yet seen Durham. The house I had bought was in Durham's Trotter Ridge subdivision and no one liked it. I chose that house because it was near Jordan High School.

As the family settled in to Durham, Ardelia resumed her teaching career. She interviewed and started teaching at WG Pearson Elementary School. Stephanie was at Jordan High and Michael went to Pearsontown. Michael had started school in Shreveport at age five and then turned six in December.

When we moved to Durham, they wanted to hold Michael back to do first grade again. Ardelia insisted on promoting him to second grade. Looking back, I think that was a mistake. Social skills tend to be slower in developing in young boys than young girls. Even today his friends are young men that are one grade behind him.

Years later Michael began to "find himself" as a maturing young adult when he was a sophomore at Norfolk State University. After returning to Norfolk that Christmas break, he decided not to register for school right away. I went to North Carolina Central University in Durham and registered him, planning for him to transfer to Durham. I called him and told him what I had done and suggested that he pack up and come home. He said he would call me back in a little while.

He called back later and said, "Dad, I'm staying. You and mom always fixed my challenges. This one I'm fixing on my own." He changed his major from Business Administration to Health Administration and returned to his coursework.

On one occasion, he was going back to school in his Nissan 240Z and was stopped for speeding. In recounting the story afterwards, Michael told me, "I did what you told me, but I almost hit him." After pulling him over, the officer had said to Michael, "Son, you know you were speeding." Michael was shocked and disrespectfully responded, "Son?! I just left my father in Durham." Thankfully, the officer just told him to move along and slow it down.

Michael's grades drastically improved after changing majors. He became a responsible young man and a highly productive professional. He is also a great husband and father today.

During my first week with the Department of Community Development, I was briefed on an unsettled relocation matter. A company was being relocated from the old Hayti community, but the relocation agreement was not finalized. The owner's daughter was coming to Durham to try to resolve the matter.

I met with the daughter that afternoon at a scheduled meeting in my office following a brief introduction by a staff member. After the meeting, she wanted to have dinner and I declined. She said she was staying at the Downtowner Hotel and if I changed my mind, I could meet her in the dining room around 8:00pm. I thanked her, and she left saying, "I will see you tomorrow at 10:00am for our follow up meeting." I went to the dining room about 6:30, had my meal and went to my room to spend some time with the relocation package, planning a way to find a way to resolve the matter the next day. I had a few drinks but was not out of control.

Around 10:00 pm, there was a knock on my door. When I looked through the peep hole, I saw tomorrow's 10:00 am appointment standing outside the door, in the rain, in her nightgown, with two glasses and a bottle in her hands. I turned and went to the phone and called the front desk and told them that one of the guests was standing out in the rain near my door. In a few minutes someone lead her back to her room and I went back to the project.

The next morning, we offered her coffee when she arrived at the office around 9:45am. I had discussed the project with the staff and was aware of the recommendation that they had presented to her and to her father, the owner. I excused the staff so that she and I could discuss the staff's recommendation. I wanted to hear her feedback.

I told her that the reason I did not have dinner with her is because I needed to prepare for my meeting with her. This was the same reason why I could not have had drinks with her. I then told her that I did not agree with the staff's recommendation. I thought that it was too generous even though it met the relocation requirements. I told her I was prepared to offer her and her father less based on stricter provisions under the relocation plan. However, if she preferred, she could choose to accept the staff's recommendation. If she did, we would pay the final relocation payment and the case would be closed. She accepted the staff recommendation which had been the offer on the table for six months, but she had been previously refusing. She thanked me and left the office.

I told the staff that you must let individuals know that you are not willing to give something that is not allowed by law. Know what you can do according to regulations. Their offer was legal but more generous than I felt was called for under the circumstances.

After six months of negotiations, they would have given most anything to get rid of her.

LIFE LESSON: Where there are laws and budget restraints, never leave yourself open for showing favoritism in business matters.

I worked for one manager in Durham that was the most non-caring person that I have ever worked with. He had a thing for one of his assistants, so she stopped going to his office alone because she was tired of his harassment.

One day he called me and said that he wanted to talk to me. He asked me to go get the assistant, let her know that he wanted to talk with the two of us. When we got there, he asked me to take something to Bahama and go over it with the Bahama Fire Department. When I left, he told me to close the door, leaving her there alone with him. I realized I had been used. When I got back, she accused me of being a participant in his harassment.

I was later promoted to the position of Assistant City Manager and the Department of Inspections and the Department of Planning were assigned to report to me instead of directly to the City Manager. I had been accustomed to having a planning staff within the community development department, but eventually I decided that wouldn't be necessary because my staff could just work with the city's planning department.

Maria was the planning director when they were moved under my oversight and I hired Paul Norby as the assistant. Maria left in less than six months and I promoted Paul to the Director position and recruited a new assistant. Paul would go on to become an outstanding director and an asset to the Durham community.

At one point, the City Manager was having trouble with Council members. One councilman came to my office and told me they were planning to trap him, because they felt he had been lying to them. At the council meeting that day, the councilman asked another council member, "What did the City Manager tell you?" When the second answered, they confirmed that he had told the two of them something completely different. The councilman looked across the Council Room at me and smiled; they went into executive session and fired the manager that night.

The City Manager had been in the process of interviewing persons for the position of public safety director and he wanted to do it before he left the city. Two candidates were being considered: the first had a regular interview of questions and answers. When the second came in, it became clear that he thought he already had the job. After some small talk, he started talking about how he was going to manage and reorganize the departments as though he already had the job.

The City Manager said to me, "I'm leaving, but the last laugh will be mine." The second candidate was part of the same political group as the councilmen who had trapped him and thought he had the job locked up. The outgoing City Manager hired the first candidate and councilmen could not do anything to change the hire.

A new City Manager took over after the last one was fired; he was an avid baseball fan. When he took his vacation, he and his wife took a trip with plans to see as many minor league baseball parks as they could in three weeks. He brought back a memento from each park that they visited. He also brought back a car trunk full of empty beer cans.

My relationship with him was a good one. I promised him that my management of Community Development would not be challenged by the fact that his wife was my assistant. She and I had a good working relationship during our brief time as Director and Assistant Director. I did not realize that after taking the position, I would be the subject of pillow talk. I didn't have a problem with my boss's wife being on my team; she had intimate knowledge of what was going on in the City.

LIFE LESSON: Put results before personalities. Determine what results you are seeking, then look around your office and decide the right person to get the job done, and get it done.

Coaching Youth Sports

In my youth, I developed a passion for athletics competition and sports. In high school and beyond, I loved the spirit of competitive sports and how relationships grew on the court and fields. I established and maintained a reputation of knowing and loving the games of football, baseball, and basketball, so I decided to coach youth sports in Durham to combine these interests with my desire to support and encourage Michael's emerging interests in sports. I became a coach in the Southwest Association Youth League.

I coached teams in football, baseball, and basketball until Michael was in ninth grade. Over the years I had the opportunity to coach kids from diverse backgrounds, skills, socioeconomic status, and very different life circumstances. We had several good teams. Our teams would play against Bethesda, Northern, and Oak Grove. I would talk to my teams before the games were about to start by saying, "You're 10 points down at the start", and the kids would play their hearts out. Once they got a ten-point lead in a basketball game I would let them settle down and enjoy the game, just playing.

I operated most of my life with the mindset that I was starting from behind and wanted to inspire these young men to play hard to get ahead not just in sports but life also. Some practice nights I would keep the team in the stands and let them talk and ask questions. I would give them the best answer that I had. If I did not know, I would say so. Michael reminds me from time to time about the time when we had a technical foul shot at the end of a basketball game that was tied. I had to put someone on the line. I chose Rocky instead of Michael. Rocky missed the shot and we lost the game. Michael reminded me on the way home that he had not missed a free shot the entire game. I think I have moved on from that bad coaching decision. Young players have a tendency to move on from a loss, but coaches tend to hang on.

Most of the kids I coached were from McDougal Terrace, Durham's largest public housing community. Jason Biggs was one of my players. I always had to have his birth certificate ready to prove his age because he was so big. He became one of the most dominant big men in the state when he went to high school and later went on to shine at a major university and later to the NBA.

I had a young man, twelve years old, nicknamed "Brad", who lived in McDougal Terrace. He was one of the best shooters and played with an attitude. I went to pick him up one morning and his little sister said, "He's not here; he spent the night at his girlfriend's". These kids had a lot of life experience for being only twelve years old.

Jason was a good athlete but wouldn't play football when he was in high school. His father is a Central Intercollegiate Athletic Association (CIAA) record setter in football at Johnson C. Smith University. Jason did not want to live in his father's shadow. Since he was also a good basketball player, he excelled there instead.

One of the most in-your-face things I did when I was coaching basketball was to enter my team in two tournaments that played at the same time. I had signed us up to play in a special Civitan Tournament, with the Southwest Conference tournament being played at the same time. My team moved into both final rounds with games scheduled on the same day, one at Lowes Grove Center and one at Bethesda Center. Start times for the games were such that the Lowes Grove game would start first, and the Bethesda game would start around what would be half time for the Lowes Grove game. This should have meant that we had to choose between which of the championship games we would participate in.

My solution was to take my entire team to play in the first game at Lowes Grove and then have an assistant coach transport six team members to Bethesda to start the second game. We won the

championship at Lowes Grove, then took the rest of the team over
to Bethesda; we arrived at halftime of that game and with the
whole team on hand won that game as well. Two championship
trophies won for one team in one day! How about that?

It was during this time that on many nights while I was sleeping,
my heart would thump in my chest, waking me up because it was
beating so fast. On more than one occasion I drove myself to a
hospital emergency room in Durham due to my heart condition,
which was diagnosed as atrial fibrillation or a-fib. I later had
four stents inserted; I still take medication to control my heart
rhythm and to keep my blood thin.

After one of my hospital stays for the heart condition, Stephanie
picked me up after my discharge. We were on the bypass heading
home and I told her to stop so I could get some beer. She argued,
but finally gave in. I bought a six pack and started all over again.
Eventually, I committed to a weekend of detox in a residential
center in the Walltown Community in Durham. When I left,
the coordinator at Walltown told me I was too educated to be
drinking like this. She gave me my valium back. I later realized
that valium is just like a dry martini.

I decided that I needed to get back in church. The first church
I saw was a local Baptist church near North Carolina Central
University. When they opened the door to the church, I decided
to join. I walked up front to join one morning. They escorted me
to a small room with others who wanted to join but I walked out

before going through with it. I felt that I wasn't ready because I was too bad, too sinful. I needed to get myself right first. Now I understand that church is a place where sinners meet to worship; we are all sinners looking for salvation. I later realized that I would not find anywhere in the Bible where God judges' sins on a curve, as though one carries more weight than another.

When one City Manager resigned to go to a city in New England, I was appointed Interim City Manager and was assisted by one assistant city manager and finance director. They both knew I was having problems with alcohol. They never said anything to me about my problem; they just did the work and I received the credit.

We had staff meeting every Monday morning and I would sit at my desk, away from the staff that was sitting in a semi-circle. I did this because I knew I smelled like an old drunk. I would not get on the elevator if others were on it because of the smell of stale beer, a smell that followed me everywhere. Even when I was struggling with being able to keep my thoughts on track, the assistant manager would finish my sentences and keep things moving in the right direction.

The City Council narrowed the manager's search down to two candidates, Orville Powell, a manager from Winston Salem, and my former manager from High Point, David Johnson. David called me one night and asked if I would speak to the Council members and give them a favorable report. I told Ardelia his request and she said, "You better not say anything good about him after the way he treated you." I did give them a favorable report on Orville.

In the spring of 1983, Council hired Orville Powell as the new City Manager. The day Orville reported to work, we had a chemical fire in Durham at SouthChem recycling plant. The City's emergency management director called me to report to the onsite command center; Orville had been notified and he arrived a few minutes after me.

As we watched the firefighters do their job and emergency professionals coordinate an evacuation plan that also involved public safety, the Red Cross, school personnel and others, Orville said to me, "This is what is satisfying to me as a manager, when you can stand back and see well trained professional government employees and others working to provide needed service to the community".

My thoughts harkened back to what Mr. P.E. Bazemore had shared with me almost twenty years earlier, "Hire someone that knows more than you about the subject, give them the freedom to succeed, never smother their creativity and they will make you look good." Orville was more than just my supervisor; he was my mentor, my coach and a cheerleader for my success. As a supervisor, he provided direction without pressure; he allowed me to grow and to expand my approach in working with all employees. I could use my managerial and supervisory skills by seeking input from all people that I interacted with.

During this time, Orville told me that he wanted me to go see Mr. Howard Clement. He did not tell me why and when I met with Mr. Clement, he asked me how he could help me. He commented on some of my problems, such as my hair and my declining ability to make presentations before the City Council. I heard him, but I did not at that time associate it with my addiction.

I did start thinking about trying to decrease my use of alcohol. I stopped drinking and started taking more Valium, a dry martini; no one ever said anything about Valium. As a matter of fact, if you had no pills left you could go to another user and get a pill to hold you over. I went to my doctor to get a refill, but he called me in and told me that he was dropping me as a patient. He did give me a refill and I left.

At the time, I was coaching a youth football team and one Saturday, we were playing a team in Orange County. I was out of Valium and began to become disoriented and confused. I had begun struggling with the basic functions of living and could not function at work. When I went home after the game, I struggled through the weekend and could not work the next week.

One Friday morning in the fall of 1983, I walked away from home; where I went and what I did I do not know. My head began to clear on Sunday as I found myself walking home coming from the direction of Chapel Hill. When I walked in the house, my mother and my brothers, Leslie and Raymond, were sitting there with Ardelia, talking about me.

I went upstairs and opened the dresser and began to drink alcohol from miniature bottles that I had collected during flying trips that were work related. At my family's request, the city nurse had secured a space for me in Fellowship Hall, a rehab center in Greensboro, N.C., but I did not want to go. Leslie said I could come with him to Raleigh, which I agreed to do.

When we arrived at his house, I was taken to a bedroom. When I lay down, my body was on fire. I could not handle the pain, so I called out to God, "God, please help me." I went to sleep and when I woke up, I called for Leslie and told him that I was ready to go to Fellowship Hall.

On our way to Greensboro, I begged Leslie to stop so I could get some beer. For a few miles, he refused but after my begging, he stopped. I went in and got some beers which I drank until I was in the parking lot of Fellowship Hall. I was petrified as I set there during the registration process. I was shown to a room and medicated where I slept through the night. The next morning when I went in the bathroom and stood in front of the mirror, my entire body started to tremble and shake. I again called on God, "Just help me." As I took my shower, I realized that something was different. My prayers before had always been something like, "God help me. If you will, I will not do that anymore." But every time, I broke my promise while He kept His. I realized that my last two calls out to God for help had no conditions attached.

God was so patient with me. This program was my first stop in finding Him for real. In counseling we talked about the journey we are all on. I had made choices to step in every mud puddle I could find along the road, but I realized the best way to get home was to go straight. When my conscience was pricked, I would just take another drink. I didn't like the man I saw in the mirror, so I would drink before shaving.

I was medicating my conscience three to four times per day. I wasn't going to church; I was living a double life. More people knew than I care to admit because I had sunk so low. At the time, I thought I had hit rock bottom.

The thing about alcoholism is that the disease itself is extremely destructive and I didn't realize that it was making things worse while I continued to allow it to control me. Alcohol gave me a mask to override the feelings of anger and pain that I was feeling inside.

When I entered Fellowship Hall, I wrote Orville to explain what was going on in my life and what I hoped to achieve through my twenty-eight-day commitment to rehabilitation. To my surprise, when I returned to work, he gave the letter back to me. I tried to read that letter and could not understand what I was trying to convey to Orville.

Subsequently, Orville became a mentor for life. At the beginning of my first full week in rehab, Orville came to see me. My fears were that I was going to be terminated or at least demoted. When he walked in the room where the counselors had taken me for the meeting, before he took a seat he said, "I do not understand this disease. I'm here to check on you to see how you are doing and to see if there is anything I or the city can do for you and your family. Now, just get well and your job will be waiting for you." What a relief!

The employment weight had been lifted from my back! I was still sick, not with alcohol, but with my stinking thinking, which I set out to change with the help of the staff of Fellowship Hall.

I attended classes and met with my assigned counselor. The most challenging task was to speak about the painful details of my drinking career. The pain that surfaced in me made me see the pain that I had caused my family and myself. I look back now and recognized that my sickness had led me to drank up a large part of my life; I realized that the only priority in my life had become the next drink.

When the inventory had to be told to someone, I chose my counselor, Jack. Telling it and hearing it out loud began with a fear of others knowing how messed up I really was. It was during my counseling session with Jack that I had to leave the Drunk behind and to find the real Cecil. To rebuild my life, I had to leave my old self behind. I knew that the beginning of a new life would take time, prayer and support from family and friends. It was during this time I knew that my garbage had seen the light of day. I was empty; my next step was to pick the tools that I would need to grow into a more loving father, a caring husband, a better friend, coworker and a compassionate supervisor.

I began to turn back to the God that I saw in my mother and father. He was the center of their lives and I began to realize that I needed that to survive.

One weekend was designated as family weekend, where family members could come and visit. Ardelia and the children came to visit. I was apprehensive about their coming, not knowing how I would be received. When they arrived, I met them in the courtyard, and we sat under a tree at a picnic table. Seeing them made me happy and it also made me feel that I was seeing them anew, that newness was because for almost thirty days I had been clean and sober. I was happy to see them yet afraid that they would reject me as a husband and as a father.

Michael was around eleven years old and he wanted to know when I was coming home. He told me about his football games and how many touchdowns he had scored and their winning record. Stephanie was not as talkative. Ardelia told me that the City of Durham was giving my paycheck to her so she could pay our bills. I could tell that she was disappointed in me and I realized that I had work to do.

Later a counseling session was scheduled for couples however, Ardelia was not able to make it. I was left to navigate my failings with her after I returned home, one on one, with no counselor to guide us. I did not rush through my past with her all at once; it took many years before I felt that I was free from my past.

The day of my discharge from Fellowship Hall in October 1983, I had no one to pick me up, my counselor told me that he would take me home. On the way, he spoke to me reassuringly. He said I would not make a recovery, because addicts do not recover. We just remain in recovery as long as we do not return to our drug of choice. He gave me the name and location of an AA meeting which he encouraged me to attend that night.

Once he dropped me off at home, I was filled with terror. Ardelia was at work and the children were at school. How would they receive me when they came home? How would my coworkers receive me when I returned to work? I saw Ardelia walking up the driveway a few hours later and I could see the pain on her face; the pain of not knowing who I was and the burden that I had placed on her all these years. The failures that she had never expected to endure.

A few months later, Ardelia confronted me one morning because she had heard that I had an affair. When Ardelia asked me if it was true, I admitted my transgressions. She began to shout, and all hell broke loose. I felt a relief that this painful truth was now out, but I did not know how to respond so I left for work.

Shortly after having arrived at my office, Ardelia arrived at my office and Orville showed her in. She continued to scold me and to point out how disappointed she was in me. She left the office after a while and went home.

I spent that night in a hotel, and I even called out to God for help and guidance. I also cried about the life that I had been living; a life of lies, pretending that I was ok, wearing a mask. Now the mask had been ripped off and I was exposed as a very flawed individual.

That night I took a mental trip back to the treatment center and the discussion I had with my counselor, Jack. In one session, he had said to me that you will not get on the road to real recovery until you expose all your past to the ones you love and make amends to all you have hurt. I thought about the personal inventory that I had done while in the Center and I made a mental note of all the people that I needed to reach out to and seek forgiveness. That process began the next day and to some extent it continues today, by having conversations with young men that I encounter that I know are living a reckless life. I know that wisdom comes with age and from knowing God, it is given to us if we seek him. Wisdom is not a thing, it is not having knowledge, but knowing God. I also know that when one gets wisdom it is to be shared. As a senior citizen I believe that I should leave this world empty, in other words share your knowledge with others.

I moved out of the hotel the next day, went to work and tried to have a normal day. Bernard Farmer, a friend, said that I could spend some time at his home. I spent one night with him and the next night, another friend, James Taborn, called and said, "I am coming to get you and take you home."

James picked me up at Bernard's and said, "Let's go." When we arrived at my house, I told him that I could not go in because I was not ready. He said, "you will never be ready. You just have to face it and go home where you belong." When we drove into my driveway, the shame, the guilt, the fear of my failing welled up in me to the extent that I was frozen until he said, "You must man up and go inside."

When I went inside, I was confronted by Ardelia and she said, "So you came back!" I went upstairs and went to one of the unused bedrooms that had twin beds; I pulled one of the beds in front of the door and prepared myself for bed. Ardelia then knocked on the door and said, "If you are going to be here, you might as well sleep in your own bed." I did not know how to take that, but I took a deep breath and went to our bed. I slept on the edge, but I remember sleeping very well that night.

From there, we began our "new normal" life. I made a decision not to talk with her about my failings; I would let her ask or express her anger whenever she was ready. For several years, she would bring it up often.

Around ten years later, she said to me, "I forgive you, but I will never forget." That statement of forgiveness stayed with me and she never mentioned my transgressions again.

She forgave me, but it took me much longer to forgive myself. I now know the power of God and His words that call us to forgive others. And we forgive so that we too can be forgiven. It took many years after she forgave me for me to forgive myself.

After two months back from Fellowship Hall, Orville called me to his office and told me that he was reorganizing the internal operations of the City Manager's office. The reorganization included promoting me to the position of Senior Associate City Manager where I would supervise the police, fire, emergency management, engineering, water resources, planning and inspection services departments and supervise two assistant city managers.

In retrospect, Orville Powell could have terminated me based on my alcohol abuse but instead he kept me on. Three months later, I was promoted to Senior Assistant City Manager. I was determined to succeed because of what Orville had done for me, something that I absolutely did not deserve.

My title was later changed to Deputy City Manager. Orville told me that day, "I give you all the authority to manage internal day-to-day affairs of the city and I (Orville) will take care of Council and the outside influences)

Orville also said if you ever do something I disagree with, rest assured that we will discuss it in private, behind closed-doors, and I will never mention it to anyone again, even you!" Over time, we did have a few closed-door meetings but they were always constructive.

Cecil Brown

As Deputy City Manager, I worked with several departments in filling senior management positions. On one occasion, a position came down to three candidates. I recommended one individual to the City Manager. He countered, "He has less tenure than the others, but I value your opinion." He asked if I would talk to one of the more senior candidates about his issues, especially since he was getting passed over for promotion on a regular basis.

I called him in my office one afternoon and we talked about his problem. I spoke to him about his coming in the building on weekends and other things that he did not think that others knew. I then recommended that he contact the city's employee assistance program. I talked to him about his story, but I really was telling him part of my story. He later got into a counseling program and was able to rebuild his life.

In my career in local government in each city, I encountered situations where management and employees could not find common ground to exist without conflict. In Durham, Josh was always in trouble with his department administration. I must admit that Josh was headstrong, however he was a very good worker. He performed his work, but he was often written up for such things as insubordination. Josh kept detailed notes of his encounters with his supervisors and filed a grievance against the department. As hearing officer, I had to conduct the hearing.

When the department presented their case, Josh countered with his position and read statements that were made to him by his supervisor that contradicted what the department presented as their case against him. His notes were dated, precise and included the times of each incident. I ruled in favor of Josh.

The department director appealed and asked for a meeting with Orville. I informed my secretary to schedule the appeal meeting, which she did. Subsequently, I had to change the meeting date because I was going to be out of town when it was scheduled. The department director scheduled another meeting with Orville behind my back in the same time slot, knowing I would not be able to be present.

In the interim, my meeting out of town was cancelled for that day, but I didn't tell the director. I asked my secretary to inform me five minutes after the meeting started. I could see the director and Josh's supervisors when they entered the City Manager's suite.

Five minutes after they entered, my secretary buzzed me and told me that the meeting had started. I went in the suite and entered Orville's office. I apologized and announced that my meeting had been postponed and then told the department director to proceed with his comments. The director finished his presentation of what he called my "failure to understand the department's position during the grievance hearing." Orville asked, "Well, what did he rule?"

The director told him my ruling and Orville said to him, "Good, Cecil made the call and it stands; he speaks for me in these hearings."

When we left Orville's office, I invited the director into my office where I proceeded to advise him to never again call a meeting about an issue concerning me behind my back. He apologized and indicated he would comply with my position.

Josh was later moved by me to head up a City Clean Team. The City Clean Team was formed after I passed by a growing pile of trash in an area of the inner-city. I passed it for two days, thinking, "Somebody needs to do something about this trash."

Then I realized that somebody was me. I went to the office and told Orville that I was going to form a team of employees to clean up trash around the city and that I wanted Josh to head up the team. I was going to ask the Director of Engineering to provide three employees that he was ready to release and one large dump truck with associated tools. I received a list of employees within two days along with the truck number and the inventory of tools.

I then spoke to the City Attorney about my plans because it also included trash on private property that was an eyesore for the city. He instructed me to allow them to enter private property if it was adjoining a public right-of-way. If legal action was taken against the city, he would gladly defend our action in court if needed.

I called Josh to my office along with the other members of the team. They all were in the dark as to why they were being asked to appear before me. I spoke to Josh alone and informed him what I was asking him to do and what his limitations were and what my expectations were of him.

I then called in the other employees and informed them of why they were called to my office. They all breathed a sigh of relief. The program was a complete success. It later evolved from not only trash collection in vacant lots but also addressing graffiti by removing it within hours of discovery.

The uniform patrol officers would notify the watch commander and he or she would contact Josh. The team was later rolled into the neighborhood services department after I left the city. The functions still exist today as part of the Sanitation Department.

LIFE LESSON: Employees not succeeding in one department might be successful elsewhere. Don't write a quality employee off just because of political challenges in their current assignment.

The Nigeria Experience

In May of 1994, Orville called me into his office and informed me that a staff member had to accompany a group of sister city community members to Kostroma, a sister city in Russia. He pointed out that it was my turn to go, but he was sending Assistant City Manager Greg Bethea. I was afforded the opportunity to accompany and participate in a three-week workshop in Nigeria instead.

Orville said that he would prefer that I go to Nigeria for two reasons: (1) I had more local government experience and I could work better with the professors from NC State University and UNC Charlotte, who were going with a grant supported by USAID. The substance of the grant was to provide information on how local governments operate in the United States and (2) The Russians drank heavily at all their functions and he did not want me to be subject to their response of my refusing to join in the toast and celebrations.

Nigeria had just had its first democratic election and the previous dictator was not elected. Before we left for Nigeria, the newly elected national government was overthrown by the former dictator Abacha. The State Department gave us the permission to follow through with the trip anyway. I went along with three professors from NC State University and three from UNC Charlotte.

We left for Nigeria on May 25, 1994. Our mission was to conduct two workshops in six cities across Nigeria. The title of our workshop was: "The Democratization of Nigeria". My role was to explain and demonstrate how local government carried out their responsibilities around each issue that the professors raised.

I had reservations about the trip. My fears showed up: fear of flying, how will we be treated, will I get sick, will Ardelia be ok, will I fall off the wagon. The list of fears continued until the plane landed in Cincinnati, Ohio, where we were to take a connecting flight. While waiting for the connecting flight to Heathrow Airport in London, I prayed to God to protect us and my family back home. I said, "Lord, I place myself and my family in your hands and I will trust and have faith in You." Once I gave it to God, I was no longer fearful, because I knew I wasn't the one in control, I was able to take a nap. When the flight was announced I boarded without fear. When we left Cincinnati, I was sitting in the middle seat of three rows of seats. The men sitting on each side of me went to sleep as soon as we were airborne. Before too long I had a head laying on each of my shoulders. A long ride and a long night.

We went to six cities in three weeks, with two sessions a day and spoke to crowded assembly halls in every city. In one city, the session was closed by the citizens loyal to the former dictator. Some cities were controlled by Muslims. We left one Muslim city with a Muslim driver and he told us that he had to get us to Ewerra and get back across the river before sunset, because Muslims were not safe in the Christian city after dark.

On the drive down, young men would pull trees across the highway to force us to stop. Once we stopped, they would approach the car and ask for a small amount of money. Once money was given to them, they would move the tree so we could pass. As soon as we would pass they would put the tree back and go back in the brush to await new victims.

On another occasion, we were stopped by the National Police carrying assault weapons and demanding money. On this occasion, we had three five-gallon containers of gasoline behind the back seat of the car. The Nigerian professor did not want to pay so they made us park the car and left us sitting beside the road. Occasionally, one would come back to the car and ask, "Have you changed your mind?" We finally convinced the professor to pay them off. Once he paid them, we were on our way.

One afternoon while waiting to start a session, one panel member was not in place. The resident professor said, "Those Ebos are always late.

When he said that, I remembered my great grandmother saying to my grandfather, "You are just like those Ebos." That night, I called my mother to ask her if she remembered grandmother using those words. She said, "Yes. Why?" I told her and she said she heard it growing up, but she never asked what it meant.

The very next day, I purchased two books on the history of Nigeria, and I found that Ebos was the name of a tribe located on the Niger River. It appears that my family might be descendants of the Ebo tribe, which is why that statement carried forward to my great grandmother's generation.

The three weeks in Nigeria was a wonderful experience. However, the most revealing and life changing experience was, when I boarded the plane in Cincinnati, I had prayed to God "to protect us from harm and danger," and I had said, "I place my care in Your hands." During the three-week trip, I do not recall a moment where I was stressed or afraid, even when we were stopped by heavily armed police or tanks in the street where the military cancelled one of our sessions. We were told that the troops were a small group of defectors that was still supportive of the ousted dictator.

When we arrived back in the United States and landed in Atlanta, I began to stress, will the plane be on time? What is awaiting me at home and at work? The list of things to worry about just grew until I was back at my previous stress level. A great deal of time had passed before I realized that I was not stressed in Nigeria where I had no control and I had given myself to God's care. I had lived three weeks without any fear or concerns.

LIFE LESSON: Let God do it; just stay out of His way.

Emergency Management

When I arrived in Durham in 1980, the city's emergency management operation was housed in the basement of the police headquarters in an old firing range. The director was a retired army major and was in the process of retiring for the second time. The department wasn't really on anyone's radar.

In 1982, the City hired Ellis Stanley to build a department that could respond to any and all disasters that could be conceived to happen in Durham, both city and county. He built the department into one of the best in North Carolina and the Southeast. He helped prepare the team for its first test, responding to a large fire at SouthChem, a major chemical recycling plant in the city.

The plan went off without a hitch, including the following: fire responders and hazardous material teams addressing the chemical fire; police closing streets and controlling traffic; warning the community to evacuate and how to do so; opening schools to shelter evacuees and providing buses to transport evacuees. The Red Cross opened their facility to provide for health and medical needs and local restaurants provided food for first responders and evacuees.

Ellis developed the first organized first responder program in Durham. He had led table top exercises involving personnel from city and county employees along with other vital agencies across the state.

Ellis later took over the emergency preparedness function for Fulton County and the City of Atlanta, Georgia. He rebuilt their emergency response function and then was hired by the City of Los Angeles, California. He was considered for the position of Secretary for the Department of Homeland Security in the Obama Administration.

When Ellis left Durham in 1985, I was given the task of hiring the next Director of Emergency Management. I discussed the current conditions and the long-term need for Durham County and the City of Durham with Ellis and asked him for recommendations on who he thought were the top four emergency management directors in the southeast. He came back to me with three names.

After interviewing the applicants, I decided to visit, and subsequently hire, William "Bill" Colley, Director of Emergency Management for Baton Rouge, Louisiana. After we hired him, Bill put in place an even stronger system that served the city and county through hurricanes and one tornado. On each occurrence, the city and county were reimbursed for all expenses from FEMA because Bill's system accurately captured all expenses related to recovery.

I was aware that other cities did not get reimbursed because they didn't have good records. Bill's talent in this area paid off for Durham. When Hurricane Andrew hit Homestead, Florida in August 1992, Bill came to me with a request from the City of Homestead asking for assistance. I asked that he put together a plan for providing help.

Two days later, he came in with a plan that included fifty-five city employees, including a mechanic, heavy trucks and several front-end loaders. The plan included the NC National Guard transporting our heavy equipment on rail cars to Homestead Florida, offloading the equipment in Homestead, and providing air transportation to Florida for city employees on military planes. City Manager Orville Powell approved the plan and we implemented it.

I went to Homestead a day in advance to arrange for living quarters for the employees. After we spoke with city leaders and the local national guard officials, they erected a tent city on a basketball court at a park playground. This provided housing for our employees with showers and a kitchen and dining facilities. The National Guard also prepared meals for the city employees.

Our city employees drove into neighborhoods filled with debris and were rewarded by grateful citizens waving and shouting thank you. The crew spent two and a half weeks removing debris. Bill had planned so well that the City of Durham was reimbursed for all our expenditures.

Our mechanic stayed busy helping all the agencies because no other out of state crews had thought to bring a mechanic. Our plan did not include an emergency medical services crew though and unfortunately, we had one employee that broke his arm. The National Guard quickly treated him and flew him back to Durham on an emergency flight. Our city employees received a warm welcome when they returned home and received praise for a job well done from Durham citizens, Council members and the County Commissioners.

LIFE LESSON: When you take your resources into disaster environments, remember to take resources to take care of the health and well-being of your personnel and mechanical support materials.

In Durham, the Department of Public Safety was both police officers and fire fighters; they were one in the same. This became a problem when the department was managed by police, who were staffing and dispersing uniform patrols for crime response. They also had to respond to fires.

One day, there was a break in at a Councilman's convenience store on the corner of Fayetteville and Pilot Street. While the police were investigating, the fire bell went off and they had to stop collecting evidence and respond to a fire call. The councilman raised hell shortly thereafter and the Council directed the City Manager to engage a consultant to study our public safety program and make a recommendation for improvement to Council.

Although we did not expect them to recommend much change, the consultant came back and recommended that we completely split the department into separate fire and police departments. Orville told me to work up a plan for a two to three-year transition to separate the two departments.

I was concerned that the election in two years would complicate things, so I suggested we pursue it expeditiously. His response was, "You can try. Let me see your plans as to how it will be accomplished."

The Human Resources Department surveyed the current officers and found that a surprising forty wanted to change to fire protection only. We finished the job in eighteen months instead of three years. This required recruitment of new police and fire fighters, as well as running two fire academies and one police academy at the same time.

There were a few small hiccups such as how to divide the money from the vending service and asking the police officers to stop hanging out at the fire stations at night, disturbing the fire fighters. These issues were also resolved.

Once the public safety department was separated into police and fire, we had to select a new fire chief for the independent department. The choice was between two assistant chiefs. The City Manager asked me for my recommendation before he talked to either of the candidates. I recommended one leader because he had been more active in the rebuilding process. Both individuals had been on the force so long that they had been part of the original black firefighters in Durham.

After Orville interviewed them he called me in his office and we discussed the two potential hires. He then told me that he felt that they were both well qualified, but he had chosen one because he felt his personality was more suited for the times that lay ahead. The other was outspoken and more direct in his approach to issues, while Orville's pick was more laid back and easy going. They both worked together very well to rebuild a first-rate department.

When Orville resigned to become a professor at Indiana University in the Department of Public Policy and Public Administration in 1997, Durham City Council appointed me as Interim City Manager. I was sworn in as the first black City Manager for the City of Durham, which lasted for one year.

While I was Interim City Manager, Council wanted to open the position to hire a permanent person for the role. One councilman told me Orville had recommended that I be appointed to that spot. One day he came to me and said, "We are going to make you City Manager." He said, "I've got seven votes out of thirteen... today's the day." I objected, "Don't do it." I felt like he was rushing things and I would be better off if I went through the hiring process, with Council considering multiple candidates.

When the Council work session opened, Councilman Martin said to Council that he had a priority item for discussion. He was given the floor by the Mayor with no objection. "Mayor, Members of Council, I place in nomination the name of Cecil Brown to be our next City Manager." The mayor asked for a second, which was made, and the floor was opened for discussion.

One of the other councilmembers looked at me with anger and I believe, with malice in his heart. He and I had attended a conference in Virginia previously and he told an official from Hampton Roads that I was going to be the next City Manager of Durham. Although he favored me for the role, he was mad that someone else had suggested it publicly instead of him. He wanted the credit for doing it. He had been a kingmaker for leaders before me, and felt he deserved credit for all of them in his role as a councilman.

The councilman who was supposed to be the seventh vote was not in Council chambers because his plane was late. Council talked for a while; the back and forth between these two men was so heated that I was asked to leave the chamber. The absent councilman never arrived. Council tabled it for the next meeting and it never came up again.

A few days later the councilman who objected called me to his office and said that if I didn't stop them from lobbying for me, he would expose my history with alcoholism.

I talked to my would-be advocates urging them to stop pushing me for the role. Council went forward with the hiring process. One councilman insisted I be considered as a candidate. I was scheduled for an interview with the search committee.

I told them, "I am withdrawing myself from consideration for the role of the City Manager of Durham, but since you have the time scheduled for me, I want to tell you some things." I proceeded to pour out all my issues with one councilman who I didn't name; they all knew who I was talking about.

The first item on my agenda as Interim City Manager was to line up the human resources I needed to lead well. I promoted John Peterson, the Finance and Budget Director to the role of Interim Assistant City Manager. I also promoted Paul Norby, the Planning Director, to the same role. Greg Bethea was already Assistant City Manager.

I split the Budget and Finance department into two separate roles with Laura Southard taking the Budget Director role and Nav Gill as Finance Director. This group made up my Management team. In my first meeting with the group I stressed to them that I wanted them to be brutally honest with me and put their thoughts and positions on issues on the table. I assured them that I would always listen to them.

The first order of business was deciding the road map for developing the annual City budget. After lengthy discussion, it was decided that we would divide the departments into three service groups; one was Public Safety, which included police, fire, emergency management and communications. We gave each group a targeted overall budget for their group. They were to first determine a group mission, group goal and objectives. Each individual department would break down the group's goal and objectives into their individual program objectives. They would work together to plan how the budget would be allocated among departments. The discussion in the three groups was spirited and rewarding.

When we took the budget before City Council each group presented that group's budget request. Of all my years in local governing, this was the first and only time I was part of an annual budget presentation to the Council that was approved in three days. The three groups presented much more quickly than when every department presented their goals and requests independently. It also made it easier for Council because the departments had worked out plans for how our service delivery to the community would work together.

Police Chief Johnson had been relieved of his duties before Orville left the City and I was given the task of hiring a new police chief. There was one chief in Charleston, SC, that came to mind, a well-known chief whose department was recognized for his department's method of policing. I contacted him, and he showed interest. I then spoke to three Councilpersons about this chief. It got out in the business community that I was speaking with this chief and even the Chamber of Commerce wanted me to bring him in. I got word that Duke University would like to add him to their roster of Adjunct Professors.

In the Monday night council meeting that followed, I asked Council for an executive session to discuss personnel matters, to which they agreed. I had a meeting scheduled with the candidate the next day and I wanted to advise Council on my progress in hiring a chief. We went into executive session and I explained to everyone about this chief.

Before I could complete my position on the matter, I was interrupted by one councilman, who said, "We do not want his kind in Durham." He proceeded to rail against the chief's hard-nosed, intense style and my desire to even consider him. One of the council persons was aware of the conversations and was even scheduled to go with me to meet with the candidate in

South Carolina the next day. While I was being blasted, he sat there silently along with all other councilmen.

After the meeting was adjourned as I was leaving, several council members came up to me and said, "He should not have blasted you like that."

My response was quick: "You had your opportunity to speak in the meeting. You said nothing then. I refrained from stating some of you knew, so do not say anything now."

The next morning, I called the Chief to tell him that I got pushback from the Council and would not be moving forward, even though I had the authority to fill the position of police chief. I was not able to fill this position during my one-year term.

On occasion during my time as the Interim City Manager, we had to make presentations to bond rating agencies of New York. One Assistant City Manager worked with the Budget Director to prepare the presentation with all the financial information that we would present to the rating agencies. The board room where we met with the agencies looked out over Wall Street, in Durham, NC and the city's statue of the Bull was in full sight. When I looked out the window and saw the bull statue, I was struck with the strong question, "How did I get here, the son of a tenant farmer?"

I made the introductions and the staff presented a detailed report on the financial strength of the city of Durham. Weeks later, the city received AAA bond ratings from both municipal bond rating agencies. That Assistant City Manager later retired from the City of Durham and moved across the state line to South Carolina working as an Assistant City Manager, then City Manager. When he took the City Manager position, he called me to thank me for giving him the opportunity to grow and develop under my leadership.

LIFE LESSON: "Being honest is a virtue; one will always fare well when doing so".

In July 1997, a new city manager was hired. He arrived in Durham after serving six years as fire chief of Oakland, California and Assistant City Manager. Three years later, he would return to his home state of California to become San Diego's Assistant City Manager. I did not like his management style. On one occasion, the manager and I were having a discussion and he told me that he was concerned about me having an open-door policy where employees could easily make appointments to see me on any matter.

If the issue was job related, my policy always was for the employees to explain the issue to their supervisor, if it was personal, they merely had to notify their supervisor that it was personal. He clearly had a different philosophy on leading the staff. I was not comfortable managing where employees were not valued no matter the position. I knew that it was time to leave an organization that I loved and I quickly called my family. I felt that it was better for me to leave because I was not willing to change my managerial style. I believe that all men are equal and a person's position in life does not make them less of a human, one of God's children. I knew that I had been mentored by the best and I did not wish to work in an environment where I would not be excited to go to work every day, so it was now time for me to move on.

HUD Community Builders

HUD was starting a Community Builders program, where they were employing individuals from across industries and governmental agencies for a two-year fellowship. Professionals would be trained to promote HUD programs across the country and assist communities and local governments in utilizing HUD programs.

In November 1998, I resigned from the City of Durham and joined the HUD Community Builder team. Orientation and training were conducted over a four-week period. Two of those weeks were spent in Washington, DC where the agency covered HUD programs and policies. This was followed by a two-week session on public policy and government training at the Kennedy School of Government at Harvard University.

Upon returning to the HUD office in Greensboro, I was assigned sixteen counties in Central and Northeastern North Carolina.

As a Community Builder, I was responsible for meeting with communities that were currently participating in HUD Programs to introduce myself and discuss additional HUD opportunities. This first year included a lot of time in my car, from Durham, NC to Elizabeth City, NC and all points in between.

When Hurricane Floyd struck North Carolina in September 1999, I was given the task of setting up and staffing a satellite HUD office in Tarboro. I had to assess the needs, prioritize them and identify personnel that would be necessary to meet the needs of the residents in Tarboro, Princeville, Rocky Mount and the surrounding areas. I then asked for volunteers from the Greensboro (NC), South Carolina and Ohio field offices. I did not receive one volunteer from the North Carolina Field Office. The NC field office director had no clue how to respond to disasters.

I selected employees from the volunteers from Ohio and New Jersey to staff the satellite office, where we served impacted residents with temporary relocation and financial assistance. This assignment lasted for nine months. I opened the satellite office in Tarboro North Carolina each morning at eight o'clock for that period, commuting nearly two hours from Durham each day.

I became a little annoyed to see the flow of Congress persons, nationally known dignitaries and others coming to tour the devastation. These became known as posturing, pontificating and picture taking sessions, but were of little help to the needs of the people in crisis. The state also experienced heavy snow storms during that winter, up to twenty-six inches in some areas. I was still commuting each day to Tarboro.

One evening the field office director called me around seven o'clock and suggested that I might want to return to Tarboro that night so that I would be available to open the office the next morning. Weather reports said there was not as much snow in the eastern part of the state. That trip was an adventure! It took over three hours when it normally took under two. The heavy snow decreased east of Knightdale.

I did not realize how many bridges I had been crossing on my daily commute until that night as I drove gingerly over each one. After my car started fish-tailing on the first bridge, I decided to take my foot off the brake, set them on the floor, and simply let my car roll across the bridges. What a night!

At the end of two years the Department of Housing Development placed all Community Builders in various departments and divisions as regular HUD staff members. I was assigned to the Office of Field Policy and Management. I was still assigned to the northeastern section of North Carolina and was responsible for filing the department's weekly report to the regional office in Atlanta, Georgia. I was also responsible to conduct grant writing workshops for nonprofits across North Carolina to help them apply for HUD funding. Some workshops were conducted in conjunction with the regional office out of Atlanta.

The Office of Field Policy and Management had no supervisory control over the field divisions located in the office so getting reportable information was difficult. Three of four divisions, Public Housing, Community Development and Equal Opportunity/ Affirmative Action reported to the district office in Atlanta. Housing reported to the central office in Washington DC.

I was astonished to find that the field office had little or no control as to how and what information was distributed to the public. Once a week, we would receive talking points on key issues which would define our standard mode of operation to address issues if we were contacted.

I was asked to speak at the dedication of a facility in Durham. This was a facility which I had been involved in the mediation and resolution of long drawn out negotiations between the neighborhood and the Federal Highway Administration when I was a new City of Durham employee in 1980. I told my supervisor and he asked me to write what I wanted to say, and he would send it to the Atlanta office to seek their input. I drafted my speech and gave it to him. He sent it to Atlanta, and I waited.

As the time drew near, I asked him about the approval but got no response. When the time arrived and I had not received the approval, I went to the dedication service and delivered my speech anyway. I received approval a few weeks after the date of the event with a few deletions and rewritten sections of my speech. I learned: they don't respond based on what you ask, they tell you only what they want you to know and what they want you to say.

I organized a quarterly congressional meeting for the North Carolina congressional staffs. The purpose was to update the congressional staff on HUD activities in the congressional districts they represented. These sessions along with regular visits to the congressional office appeared to be positive events for the congressional staff.

It was during this time that my daughter introduced me to a church that was holding services in an old supermarket space in Durham. She said that the congregation was composed of people, both young and old, so I decided to attend. After my first visit, I was convinced that this was the place for me.

This was the beginning of a new chapter in our lives and became a source of restoration for my soul. The praise and worship services captured my heart. The preaching was all Bible based which lead me to become an avid reader and eager student of the Bible. This really changed my focus in my spiritual walk. I enjoyed the worship and Bible teaching so much that I took notes. I would go back and look over them later in the week to refresh the teaching and increase my level of understanding. The church moved to its new location and after a few months, Ardelia and I joined the church. I joined the Usher Ministry and Ardelia joined the Children's Ministry.

Historic Properties, LLC

While at HUD, Ardelia was diagnosed with Alzheimer's. This diagnosis started us on a new and very uncharted journey. I knew that I had to get closer to home to support her, so I chose to look for work in Durham. There was a developer who specialized in historic properties who would often visit HUD. He had used HUD programs in renovation of historic properties in North Carolina. I had met him previously during my time as an employee with the City of Durham.

I spoke to him one day while he was at the Greensboro HUD office and told him that I was ready to get off the road and would love to work for him out of his Durham office. A few weeks later, he called me and asked if I was serious about changing jobs and I said, yes. He then asked if I could meet him for a discussion of some possibilities one afternoon on my way home. We agreed to meet at the Downtown Tower in Durham. I met with him and one of his associates.

We talked for at least an hour as he laid out all the plans and as he spoke, I could see myself finishing my work career with this company. I was offered a part time position working thirty hours a week as an independent contractor. A few days later, I called and accepted his offer. I felt that I could make an impact in this area and still be home to take care of Ardelia when the full-time need arrived.

The new job started off crazy! The office space was not what I was told it would be. We were working from an apartment unit in the Center Village Apartments. I was the second team member, working thirty hours a week and pay periods were scheduled for the fifteenth of the month. When the fifteenth came, they asked me if I could wait until the thirtieth to get paid. The owner did not ask me himself he sent his associate who told me the owner was having money problems.

In less than three months, I was asked to take on a full-time position, which I accepted. We then hired a full-time bookkeeper. Her initial role was to stabilize the accounting system so it would stand up to an auditor's review. She never got this done because the owner was so "flexible" with the accounts; he was a manager like no other manager that I had ever witnessed.

Market studies were completed on the Augusta Arsenal in New Jersey; a historic military arsenal built in 1828. The Augusta Arsenal is a majestic site. After the market studies were completed and financial partners signed on, state tax credits were approved by the legislature. Funding for the project later became difficult to secure and the project floundered. The struggle for construction funding goes on as of this writing. Another development, "The Factory" was developed into a commercial, residential and medical complex in Jersey City.

On one occasion, I was dispatched to Augusta, Maine to attend the annual meeting of the Chamber of Commerce. My orders were to report that the property would be developed. I was selected to go because the owner knew the Chamber had issues with him. One member said to me that I did not lie like him.

I was concerned that the financial plans had no logic; it was a hit or miss proposition. Despite my concerns, I delivered the message to the Chamber with a projection that I knew was not realistic. I did not want to take the trip, because I was scheduled to attend the A&T homecoming game that Saturday. I flew up on Thursday evening, the meeting was Friday at noon, and I was to fly out of Newark at 5pm Friday afternoon.

As usual I was pulled out of the check-in line for additional screening on the way back. It always happened to me at the out of the boarding line at the Airport. After checking in, we were notified that the flight to Raleigh/Durham (RDU) had been cancelled and that was the last direct flight for the night. I was then ticketed on a flight to Atlanta and from Atlanta to RDU. The arrival time for RDU on that schedule was to arrive at 3:30 am Saturday.

When I boarded the plane to Atlanta, I was seated in an aisle seat with the window seat vacant. The plane was almost full and about to push away from the gate when a woman entered the plane. As the flight attendant assisted her down the aisle, she pointed to the seat beside me. My disappointed thoughts were, "Oh my, I thought I was going to relax and maybe take a nap thanks to that empty seat."

When the plane reached 33,000 feet, I decided to ask her where she was from. She told me she was from Trenton and that she was going to Florida to see her son who was in the hospital with life threatening injuries from a motorcycle accident. She had just been discharged from the hospital herself over objections from her doctor. She said that her husband was in Florida by her son's bedside and she just had to get there because they did not think he was going to live. I was first overcome with how I could have been so self-absorbed before she arrived on the plane and immediately I was overcome by the Holy Spirit. Out of my mouth came the words, "Do you mind if I pray for you, your son and your family?" She spoke to me and said, "Please do." I reached for her hand and began to pray softly then later louder until persons around us could hear me praying. When I finished, we sat back and talked. I felt in my spirit that her son would be alive and waiting for her when she arrived which I shared with her.

I was reading a book with daily readings and I gave it to her to hold on to it and to study the passages that touched her heart.

She was flying through, so when I got off in Atlanta, I hugged her and told her to be strong.

I boarded my flight to RDU and arrived home around 4:00 a.m., took a nap, got up, got Ardelia dressed and went to Greensboro for A&T's homecoming. I have thought about that "chance meeting" often. I know now that it was not "chance" because it was God's plan that we met. So that I would come face to face with my selfishness and provide a word from Him to a mother in distress. I know now, and I fully understand that God's plan for me is revealed each day, not all at once, but in due time.

The owner was extremely erratic, he would on a few occasions give me an assignment, such as developing personnel policies for the business, policies such as time and attendance, vacations, offices hours, and sick leave. Once I had developed the policies and procedures, I scheduled a meeting with him to review a development. When I gave him the file, he opened it and his response was "these are good but we will not be needing them." The truth was seldom a part of his way of conducting business. He would tell potential investors that things were great when the staff knew that it was not true.

Once he sent me and another employee to fly to New Jersey to interview applicants to work on the Jersey projects. During the first interview we discovered that he had already offered the job to one woman but sent us to interview her and another candidate. We recommended the second candidate who was more qualified to perform based on our needs. He chose to hire both, but within a year they were both terminated because of the lack of funding.

He also hired a lady that was an elected official, although he did not have a specific role in mind for her when he hired her. He made a trip to New Jersey once while she was busy on government business and demanded a meeting with her. She could not make time to meet with him because of her legislative responsibilities; yet she was getting paid while not working, and I still was not getting paid.

I was given the task of flying to New Jersey to terminate her for lack of job performance. I was given a ticket to fly to Jersey, but I was only able to reach the airport in Philadelphia, even though I was running from one terminal to another trying to make connecting flights. Due to severe weather, flights were being cancelled and I was not able to get to New Jersey. I spent the night in the airport and flew back to Durham the next morning and then called her to terminate her services.

At this time, I was Chief Operating Officer of the company. (Historic Properties, LLC) While the owner was getting options on an additional property in Winston-Salem, an associate was closing a deal on a property in New Jersey. We restored this property before I left the company. This was the only property that we completed while I worked for the company.

On one morning, I went to work with the ground being covered with snow and ice. The parking lot was a sheet of ice. I got out of my car, took a couple of steps and fell hitting the back of my head on the ice. When I got in the office, blood was running down my head, neck and face. I went downstairs and the security officer called EMS. I was taken to the hospital where it was determined that I had a concussion. I stayed home for a few days.

Once the bottom fell out of the construction economy, the handwriting was on the wall that the office was closing. Associates had found employment with another company and I had no real work to do. The office was moved over one weekend and I was not given a key to the new office. I was always the first person to get to work opening the office in the mornings.

The Monday morning after the move, I went to the rental office to get a key and was told that my name was not on the list. I called the owner he told them to let me in, but not to give me a key. He never really spoke to me about anything and I was becoming very angry about all the promises that were made when he didn't follow through on any of them.

I had developed organizational policies and was preparing reports for distribution to his lenders. I later found there were not being used at all after I attended a meeting with him and several of his shareholders. I listened to the questions being asked and the answers that were given and knew then that reports were not being given to these individuals. His approach appeared to be,

I can baffle you with smoke and mirrors, because I am smarter than you.

The bookkeeper finally gave me a key to the office. At this point, they owed me over $30,000 in back pay which was six months without a pay check from this business. The owner was in negotiations with a family member for a loan. He would tell me how the discussions were going and end with, "I will pay you soon; just stick with me." The bookkeeper told me that the debt to me was not a part of the document that he sent to his potential lender. She said she had asked him why it was not included and that his response was that, "We will have to make other arrangements for Cecil."

Around this time, I had decided that it was time for me to retire and go home. The work situation was making me bitter and believing that I was not valued as an employee. Furthermore, it was obvious that my wife needed me home with her. Each morning before I would leave for work, I would help her with her bath, get her dressed and prepare her breakfast. We would go to the sunroom and have breakfast and share a few moments before I left for work. I would kiss her on her forehead and then leave for work. I would come home at lunch time and she would be sitting in the same spot where I had left her upon going to work earlier. When I came home at the end of the day, she would get up and start moving around. I realized that she was afraid or confused when I wasn't there; it was time for me to go home.

God had given me steady employment for forty-five years, even with all my imperfections as an employee, supervisor and as a manager. A few days later the owner found the nerve to call me outside and began trying to tell me that he needed to put me on leave because he was having trouble paying me and things were very tight. I then told him that I would be retiring at the end of the month which was a few days away. I asked him about my back pay and he said he would give me two thousand dollars now and that I he would get the balance to me later. I then drew up a promissory note for $28,000 which he signed with the bookkeeper as witness.

I was given a check when I left for the day. When I went to deposit it the next day, I was told that the check would not clear. I called the bookkeeper and she said he knew that there was no money in that account and that he had just wanted me to leave. She then wrote me a check for five hundred dollars. I was then left with the company owing me $29,500. It took me almost three years to close my account. I eventually closed the dispute with a much lower settlement because I was sick and tired of fooling with him.

Alzheimer's

Once I was at home full time, I tried to be both husband and caregiver, but it did not take me long to realize that the two cannot coexist in one man's body without a lot of conflict. The husband role had to take a backseat, because the caregiver role was the most important. The husband in me was a man that engaged in discussion of the world around us; the husband and wife made plans together, and we loved each other together. We both served in the church together until she was no longer able to attend. Due to the progression of Alzheimer's, she was not able to engage and follow the service.

While serving as an usher, I had become involved with the role; talking with members and making friends with pastors, who eventually began stopping by my home to check on Ardelia and me. I found myself in constant prayer for Ardelia. I asked God for help and guidance and how I might serve His child during her most challenging times. I had worked on a job for someone else for forty-five years, yet found the job as a caregiver to be the most difficult and challenging job I have ever had.

My days were always busy, but I took it in stride. I kept telling myself that she was one of God's children and I was called to take care of her. I must say sometimes I forgot my role and found myself responding to her as a spouse. I later realized that the spouse role no longer existed, so I became a full-time caregiver. That was a difficult position to take, as I realized the plans we had made for an enjoyable retirement were not going to happen.

Lesson Learned: We have to play the hand we are given.

As I continued my role as spouse and caregiver conflicts were inevitable. As it happened, I decided to take Ardelia to her hometown in Eatonville, Florida for two weeks to spend time with her ninety-three-year old mother and to attend a football game on Labor Day. We flew down on a Sunday and picked up a rental car and drove to her mother's home. We spent the day there and that afternoon I told her that it was time to go to the hotel where I had a suite reserved. She looked at me and said, "I want to go home."

I tried to explain that we were staying and that we had no reservations to fly back today. She kept saying, "I want to go home." I finally got her to the hotel and once we were checked in and arrived at our room, she would not go in... she stood in the hall telling me she wanted to go home. After some time, I got her to enter the room although she was still saying, "I want to go home."

I decided that if I forced her to stay, I would be miserable for two weeks and she would not even remember that she had been to Florida. I picked up the phone and made reservations to fly back to Durham the next afternoon. Monday morning, we got up early, rushing to make sure we got to the airport on time, turning in the rental car and moving though the airport with two large suitcases and Ardelia tagging along behind.

When we entered the terminal Ardelia would stop regularly, holding conversations with strangers and looking in store windows. I was reminded how our children would become distracted by their surroundings and would forget the task at hand. Then it occurred to me, my "two-year-old" was at her best, which helped me get through that day.

We arrived home and a friend picked us up from the airport. She asked Ardelia a few minutes after we entered the house about our trip to Florida. Ardelia looked at her and asked, "What do you mean? I have not been to Florida."

Leaving the house for Ardelia became quite an adventure because of her fear. It is so hard to see a loved one slip away. The physical person remains, aging slowly, while the mind regresses from a highly functioning adult to a very young child. I thank God for her, and I was committed to honor my vows… in sickness and in health.

One day we were at a local mall, and she was looking at clothes in a store. After a few minutes I stepped outside. Ten minutes later she came out the door with fear obviously on her face. She was lost when she realized she didn't know where I was. When she saw me outside her face changed into a big smile.

In March of 2015, Ardelia came down with pneumonia on a Saturday morning. When my niece Shirley noticed that she was lying in a fetal position and trembling, she asked for a thermometer and I could not find one. I went to the corner drug store and bought a thermometer. To our surprise she had a temperature of 104 degrees. I called the EMS and she was transported to Duke Regional Hospital where she was diagnosed with pneumonia and a mass in her right lung and blood clots in her leg.

They put a blood filter in her right leg which caused it to swell. When she was discharged, she was unable to walk and she was sick. We decided to go to our daughter's home in Wake Forest, because she had more space for the hospital bed, which we felt would be best for Ardelia at the time. Our daughter also arranged to have a single bed for me beside Ardelia's hospital bed. We all felt a little more at ease with this move as we would have a doctor in the house, our daughter, Stephanie.

Stephanie reminded me that Ardelia's condition was very serious. We began to have morning prayer next to her bed. We realized that the real doctor was and is God. As time went slowly by, Ardelia's digestive system began to stabilize and she began to eat again. Her personality began to shine through once again. She was back but could not walk; her speech was marred with incomplete sentences.

From March 2015 until December 2017, I was by Ardelia's bedside every day. For two years and ten months, I was there. I wanted to be able to see and hear her anytime during the night if she needed anything. Although she was not able to talk in complete sentences, she was my life; we had known each other for fifty-seven years and we were married for fifty-five years and eight days. Ardelia passed away on December 23, 2017.

After she passed away, I found a section marked in one of her prayer books that talked about sorrow and death happening for every believer and how hard it is to go on after losing a loved one. This section that she had marked went on to remind me that we have reason to hope, despite our sadness.

My journey continues here on earth and I have faith that I am heaven bound, to not only meet my heavenly Father but to dance with my wife again. Even though she is not physically with me, she will always be in my heart and her voice will always ring in my head as I continue to navigate the road to glory.

I have two children and two grandchildren that I can talk to, they make me smile and puff out my chest with pride when I see her in them. I continue with her spirit as my partner, leading me on the road to glory. I am walking on, but not alone. The journey is not over until God says it is over.

Endnotes

My Church and my faith keep me going. I do not worry, and I am often not afraid. But I have learned that everything we need to know is in the Bible, words such as:

Luke 12:22-31, NIV – "Then Jesus said to His disciples: 'Therefore I tell you, do not worry about your life, what you will eat; or about your body, what you will wear. For life is more than food, and the body more than clothes. Consider the ravens: They do not sow or reap, they have no storeroom or barn; yet God feeds them. And how much more valuable you are than birds! Who of you by worrying can add a single hour to your life? Since you cannot do this very little thing, why do you worry about the rest? Consider how the wild flowers grow. They do not labor or spin. Yet I tell you, not even Solomon in all his splendor was dressed like one of these. If that is how God clothes the grass of the field, which is here today, and tomorrow is thrown into the fire, how much more will he clothe you—you of little faith! And do not set your heart on what you will eat or drink; do not worry about it. For the pagan world runs after all such things, and your Father knows that you need them. But seek His kingdom, and these things will be given to you as well.'"

John 16:33, NIV – "I have told you these things, so that in Me you may have peace. In this world, you will have trouble. But take heart! I have overcome the world.

Romans 5:3-5, NIV – "Not only so, but we also glory in our sufferings, because we know that suffering produces perseverance; perseverance, character; and character, hope. And hope does not put us to shame, because God's love has been poured out into our hearts through the Holy Spirit, who has been given to us."

Romans 8:28-29, NIV – "And we know that in all things God works for the good of those who love Him, who have been called according to His purpose. For those God foreknew, He also predestined to be conformed to the image of His Son, that He might be the firstborn among many brothers and sisters."

Philippians 4:13, NIV – "I can do all things through Him who gives me strength."

The Christian life does not make us immune to life's trials and tribulations. I know we sometimes ask the question: "Why? Why would God allow us to go through such things as the death of a child, disease and injury to ourselves and our loved ones, worry and fear?" The Bible clearly teaches that God loves those who are His children, and He "works all things together for good" for us. (Romans 8:28) Trials develop godly character, and that should enable us to "rejoice in our sufferings, because we know that suffering produces perseverance; perseverance produces character; and character produces hope. And hope does not disappoint us. God has poured out His love into our hearts by the Holy Spirit, that lives in us."

Printed in the United States
By Bookmasters